brilliant

coaching

brilliant

coaching

second edition

How to be a brilliant coach in your workplace

Julie Starr

Prentice Hall
is an imprint of

Harlow, England • London • New York • Boston • San Francisco • Toronto • Sydney • Singapore • Hong Kong
Tokyo • Seoul • Taipei • New Delhi • Cape Town • Madrid • Mexico City • Amsterdam • Munich • Paris • Milan

PEARSON EDUCATION LIMITED

Edinburgh Gate
Harlow CM20 2JE
Tel: +44 (0)1279 623623
Fax: +44 (0)1279 431059
Website: www.pearson.com/uk

First published in Great Britain in 2008
Second edition published 2012

Pearson Education is not responsible for the content of third-party internet sites.

ISBN: 978-0-273-76242-3

British Library Cataloguing-in-Publication Data
A catalogue record for this book is available from the British Library

Library of Congress Cataloging-in-Publication Data
Starr, Julie.
  Brilliant coaching : how to be a brilliant coach in your workplace / Julie Starr.
  -- 2nd ed.
    p. cm.
  Includes index.
  ISBN 978-0-273-76242-3 (pbk.)
  1. Employees--Coaching of. 2. Employee motivation. 3. Management.
  I. Title.
  HF5549.5.C53S73 2012
  658.3'124--dc23
                                              2011033608

10 9 8 7 6 5 4 3 2 1
15 14 13 12 11

Set in Plantin 10/14pt by 30
Printed in Great Britain by Henry Ling Ltd, at the Dorset Press, Dorchester, Dorset

Contents

About the author

Julie Starr is a coach and consultant with over 20 years of experience of working to promote change in business. Her methods, models and approaches are used to develop great coaching practice around the world. The founder of Starr Consulting, she develops applications of coaching that make an impact on both the individual and the organisation.

She is author of *The Coaching Manual* (Prentice Hall, 2010) which defines the principles and practices of personal coaching. As well as regular speaking engagements, Julie consults and provides coaching to leaders of organisations in the UK, Europe and USA. To find out more, check out **www.starrconsulting.co.uk**

Acknowledgements

There are many people who have contributed to the development of the ideas in this book. In particular, I'd like to acknowledge the work of the following people: Richard Bandler, Brandon Bays, Frank Daniels, Milton H. Erickson, Mike Fryer, Daniel Goleman, John Grinder and Eckhart Tolle.

I would also like to thank Xanthe Wells, who was invaluable as my writing coach during the preparation of this text.

Further resources

For a reading list and other useful resources, check out **www.starrconsulting.co.uk**

Introduction

As a way of helping others learn, perform and succeed, coaching is now mainstream. It's also versatile: coaching principles can be applied in many different environments and situations. There are sports coaches, writing coaches, voice coaches and financial coaches. It seems that wherever we want to get better at something, there's a coach willing to help us. This book focuses on one distinct application of coaching: coaching in the workplace. In particular, this involves coaching that helps others perform well in their job or role at work, while increasing their skills or learning.

There may be many reasons why you have picked up this book. Perhaps you're interested in knowing what coaching is and want to explore its potential for you. Maybe it's a skill you'd like to develop further and you want practical tools or techniques that you can apply. Or maybe coaching fits into what you do already, or is part of something you'd like to do in the future. Whatever your reasons, I'll say welcome. Your interest benefits us all, because when you become a better coach for others, your contribution in your workplace increases. So to help you get the most out of the book, let's take a brief look at how the book is designed to work.

About this book

The book is split into four parts:

- Part 1: Awareness
- Part 2: Ability
- Part 3: Application
- Part 4: Action

Here's an overview of how each of these parts will help you learn and apply coaching for yourself.

Part 1: Awareness – what is coaching and how does it work?

The first part of this book explains coaching in the context of an organisation or your workplace. You'll find clear definitions of what coaching is, and what it is not. We'll also examine what it means to be a manager or leader who coaches others, and what it takes, in terms of your mindset. By reflecting on your own role, situation and challenges, we'll help you frame your own thinking and decide how coaching can work for you.

I will often talk to you as though you already are a manager and/or a leader. Please know that you do not have to have the formal role of manager to benefit from the ideas in this book. If you work in an environment where you regularly interact with others, then the technique of coaching can benefit you. If you are in a role where helping others to work better or to be more engaged and effective would really help (them or you), I'm confident that coaching has something to offer.

Part 2: Ability – what are the skills you need to develop?

In the second part of the book we'll examine the key skills you'll need to develop, such as effective questioning and giving feedback. Many of these skills are relevant outside managing or coaching situations, as interpersonal or general life skills. We'll look at how these skills work in practice, through samples of dialogue or real-life examples. We'll also examine ways to build on the ability you already have with exercises or routines to try out. Most of these exercises can be done 'undercover', so nobody needs to know what you're doing!

Part 3: Application – how can you use coaching in your workplace?

In the third part we'll look at principles and structures that will help you apply your coaching skills in the workplace. We'll explore the different ways you can use coaching as you get on with the job in hand: whether that's in formal, planned coaching sessions, or coaching 'on the hoof' as a natural response to everyday questions from your colleagues. Of course, your coaching needs to get at least as good, and preferably better, results than you're used to, before you'll adopt it in practice. So here you'll find fresh perspectives on familiar situations, where coaching principles can really help. For example, we'll explore how adopting a simple coaching response can quickly create progress on a task or issue, while helping someone to think and learn for themselves.

Part 4: Action – how can you take your learning forward?

The final part encourages you to think about what happens next, to progress your journey of learning. We'll look at simple things you might do to maintain a focus on coaching and sustain the momentum you've gained through reading the book. We'll use coaching principles and questions to help you integrate coaching behaviour in your workplace; perhaps by reflecting on what your immediate opportunities to coach are or by acknowledging what might still be blocking the way. By preparing yourself for the journey ahead, you'll be ready to tackle issues, spot opportunities and apply the tools and techniques in this book to make a real difference to you and your workplace.

Brilliant toolkit

Along the way, you'll also notice bite-sized inserts intended to support your practice and learning. This is your toolkit and it consists of the following.

 Questions

These are a series of questions to help coach your own learning and link ideas specifically to your own situation. You can choose to write your answers down, speak them out loud, or just pause and think them through. The important thing to remember is that the questions are intended to provoke thought and action, just like a coach does in a coaching conversation. So by focusing on your responses to these questions, you're letting the book go to work for you.

 Exercises

These exercises will help deepen your understanding, by applying principles or behaviours to real life. You'll be asked to try something out, often in an everyday situation, such as a conversation or meeting. Please take the time to try some of these, as only in the 'doing' will you really reap the benefits of some of the simple principles on offer.

 Tips

Here you'll find handy hints or advice to help you to get to grips with the key points of a situation. For example: the main dos and don'ts of giving effective feedback, or what to avoid when agreeing actions or next steps. Like the rest of the toolkit, the tips form a quick visual reminder that you can reference afterwards.

Checklists

The checklists will help you to plan for a situation and make sure that you're feeling prepared and well equipped. For example, this could be when tackling a tough conversation or preparing to run a meeting according to coaching principles. By encouraging you to think and prepare a little in advance, you should save headaches later. The checklists will remind you of key points or principles, at a useful point in your reading.

 Definitions

In the definition boxes jargon is busted and 'buzzwords' are foiled, as you find clear and concise meanings to commonly used terms. For example, the difference between coaching and mentoring, or what we mean by the term 'facilitation'. Often all that's needed is to confirm what you already suspected! You may be surprised by what you already know.

Getting the most from this book

This book can be read from front to back, in full or in part, or you may choose to cherry-pick from key ideas that most interest you. Maybe you're interested in lists of effective coaching questions, or want a fresh perspective on listening. Or perhaps you sometimes avoid giving feedback and want to find comfortable ways of doing that. And whatever your preferred approach to learning is, I hope to support you with your current challenges and goals. So, without delay, let's look first at what coaching is, and why it's such a great skill to have in your workplace.

PART 1

Awareness

CHAPTER 1

What is coaching?

This chapter will explain what coaching is, how it works, and – importantly – how it can work for you. We'll examine key differences in a coaching conversation and also the benefits that adopting a coaching style can bring. We'll look at the difference of influencing others by being directive, or by being non-directive. Then you'll be asked to reflect on your own influencing style, to highlight immediate opportunities for improvement.

What is coaching in the workplace?

Coaching is a conversation, or series of conversations, that one person has with another. The person who is the coach intends to produce a conversation that will benefit the other person (the coachee) in a way that relates to the coachee's learning and progress. Coaching conversations can happen in different time-frames and in different environments. For example, you might coach someone during a quick chat at the coffee machine or in a more formal meeting setting where you need to discuss something at length.

Whether a conversation constitutes coaching or not is more about the style of the conversation than its location, length or content. A coaching conversation might last two minutes or two hours since, ultimately, coaching is defined by its impact. Consider this example: I might lecture someone for an hour on what I think they should do in a situation, and they may rightfully choose to ignore me. Or I may ask a simple yet challenging question, such as 'What's really holding you back here, do you think?' In turn, this may make them realise something that previously lay hidden. The second example has more of a coaching effect, because it causes the person to think and, therefore, come to their own conclusion.

The clues to whether a conversation is a coaching conversation are:

- Is the focus of the conversation mostly on the individual being coached?
- Is the intention of the 'coach' positive towards the person being coached?
- Are the skills of listening, questioning and reflection used?
- Will the individual think about the conversation afterwards, and benefit from that reflection?
- Does the conversation benefit the thinking, learning or actions of someone in some way?

 **questions**

Where could you coach more?

Use the following to consider the opportunities you already have to coach others.

- Ⓠ How often do people ask you questions about their work and expect you to give them solutions or advice? For example, 'How do I do this?' or 'This has happened – what shall I do?'
- Ⓠ Do you feel 'indispensable', i.e. would the place fall to pieces if you weren't there to look after everyone?
- Ⓠ If someone comes to you with a problem, do you help them by giving them your thoughts, or by helping them with theirs?

If it helps, get someone you trust to reflect on your answers. You never know, you might be coaching more than you thought!

The best judge of whether a conversation had a coaching effect is the person being coached, rather than the person trying to coach them. Coaching can often be catalytic, provoking deeper thought or a richer appreciation of a topic. Whether the person experiencing the conversation would have had those thoughts, insights or ideas without that particular conversation is often best decided by them alone.

Why does coaching at work *work*?

Coaching works by increasing the *performance* of people. Where a business's success depends on the results of the people who work within it, coaching is a huge opportunity. It is now no longer enough to be a talented or expert individual – especially where you hold the position of a manager. Organisations now want 'expert individuals' to be able to develop talent and results from others: but not by increasing the controls upon them or by monitoring them more closely. In fact, coaching sometimes looks almost like the opposite of that, as the amount of control exerted by the manager relaxes. The amount by which that control relaxes is ultimately up to the manager, as Chapter 7 (A flexible style of influence) demonstrates. Managers who coach listen a little more closely, ask a few more questions and generally encourage others to think and act for themselves. In this way, coaching managers help others to stay effective over time by supporting them to learn general skills that sustain them. A bit like teaching a hungry man to fish, it's an ongoing solution.

> managers who coach encourage others to think and act for themselves

brilliant definitions

Direct report

Someone who reports to you directly, i.e. there is no other manager or supervisor between you on a reporting line or structure chart.

▶

Subordinate

Someone who is less senior to you in the organisation; they have a less responsible role or lower-graded position, etc. In this book the term is used to mean the same as a direct report (above).

Colleague

Anyone you work with, including direct reports, subordinates or people senior to you within the organisation.

Team member

In this book the term is used to indicate a member of a team that reports to you. This assumes that you are managing a team; if you're not, that's fine, simply imagine that you are. Logically, the team members we'll discuss are also your direct reports, subordinates and colleagues.

Peer

This is someone on the same level as you; their role is regarded as equivalent to your role in terms of its responsibility, grade, place in the hierarchy, etc. Remember that while we consider all *people* as equal we acknowledge that sometimes the *roles* they perform are judged to have greater or lesser values within organisations, often because of the responsibility or purpose of the role.

How does coaching at work *work*?

When we coach someone we assume that they have the ability to work things out for themselves with a bit of encouragement. So we ask questions like: 'What are your options?' or 'So, what needs to happen?' or 'What do you want to do?' That simple shift, from giving advice to asking someone what they are going to do, is at the heart of coaching as a management style.

Engagement beats compliance

One of the benefits of this shift is that when people work things out for themselves they are more engaged in the solution. Typically, if we tell someone to do something, and it doesn't work out, they might feel less responsibility for its failure. For example, I tell Geoff to get everyone who is involved in a work issue together for a meeting, so that we can agree a solution. But when Geoff tries to arrange the meeting, it's tough to get everyone together on the same day. If it's not Geoff's idea in the first place, he's less likely to look for ways to turn the situation around. On the other hand, if it was actually Geoff who suggested the meeting, he will be reluctant to want to come back with the news of its failure. Instead he is going to look for ways to overcome potential barriers, rather than deliver the news, 'It's not possible – everyone's too busy.'

> when people work things out for themselves they are more engaged in the solution

Offer empowerment not advice

Other benefits of getting people to think and decide for themselves include increasing their sense of responsibility for their issues. As people are provoked to be more responsible, gradually their confidence increases – and so does their sense of empowerment (ability to act).

Directive or self-directed – what's the difference?

Coaching in the workplace demands that we adopt a less directive style of influencing or managing others. Literally, that means that managers choose to give less advice and fewer answers, trusting that people often know what they need to and can direct themselves pretty well. Managers encourage people to form their own thoughts and views about a situation, by coaching them in a conversation.

When a manager coaches their colleagues, they are encouraging them to be self-directed. This demands that we operate from a different set of principles: instead of 'I know how' the manager needs to trust that 'you know how'. Figure 1.1 illustrates these two different ways of influencing people to do things.

Figure 1.1 Spectrum of influence

Here's how the two styles sound, as a manager talks to a subordinate.

Manager is directive	Manager encourages self-direction
You need to phone Bob and get him involved in this.	OK, right, I understand, so what do you need to do?
This is an issue with planning again; we just don't seem to be able to estimate timescales accurately.	This is a fairly frequent issue, isn't it? What do you think is causing it?
Well, I suspect it would work a bit better if you maybe wait for a week. Let people get used to the idea.	OK, what's the best plan to communicate this, do you think?

Isn't coaching just tea and sympathy?

You'll notice in the above examples that both styles have no dependency upon 'tone' or 'niceness'. Indeed it's possible to be really 'nice' and *highly directive*: for example [soft tone], 'Look, this is a really difficult situation, isn't it? Why don't you get everyone together and I'll open the meeting for you ... maybe set the scene a little.' The manager is obviously being nice, warm and supportive – and also directive. They've just given an instruction, based on an assumption that they 'know best'. A subtle shift of responsibility for the issue has taken place, since the manager has stepped in to help. They've also offered to 'rescue' the subordinate and therefore made a 'victim' out of them. The meeting may be a great idea; it's simply that the subordinate wasn't involved in thinking things through or coming up with a plan. That's what makes the manager's style directive.

brilliant tip

Cynicism is the start of belief

If you're even slightly cynical about coaching, I welcome your reservations. Quite often your cynicism is simply a need to find that something's true for you. My task is not to convince you of something I think is true, but to help you reveal *your* truth about yourself and how you work with other people. It's up to you to decide which bits of the information contained in this book will work for you. Once you've discovered something for yourself, it becomes *yours*, not mine, or anyone else's.

Coaching is not by definition 'nice' or 'soft' – it can actually be very challenging. A manager can influence others in a less directive way, while being pretty punchy. For example [strong tone], 'Yes, right, so I understand absolutely what you're saying, I just need to know what you've decided to do ...' Here the manager is acknowledging they've heard what's happening and is challenging the subordinate to come up with an answer. You might not like the mildly aggressive tone, but that's not the point. The key thing to remember is that this manager is encouraging, or maybe even forcing, a subordinate to 'own' both the situation and its solution. That's what makes it a less directive style. Sometimes a less directive style can put a subordinate under more pressure in a situation as they are placed in a clearer position of responsibility. The manager's role is to judge whether or not that's something that is constructive and helpful in the situation.

Tough guy or teddy bear? – A coach can be either

How much warmth is needed depends on the person and the situation. In the end you'll decide for yourself. But let's be clear that while coaching can be warm, encouraging and friendly, it isn't defined by those terms. What's more important is that the person you are coaching is engaged in the conversation with you. Some people are actually 'turned off' by a friendly style and would prefer 'straight talking'. Only you can decide what will work best for you and the people or situations you deal with. Flexibility is the key, as your ability to adapt to the needs of people and situations enables you to tackle things in a variety of ways. We'll deal more with this topic later, in the skills outlined in Part 2.

> how much warmth is needed depends on the person and the situation

 brilliant definitions

Mentor

A mentor gives relevant opinions or advice because their own professional experience matches yours in some way. So a mentor is more of a 'wise guide' because of their relevant skills or knowledge. Generally, a mentor is more involved in the *content* of a conversation, whereas a coach is more focused on the *process* of it.

Coach

A good coach can coach most people in most situations, because they are able to support a person's own thinking processes, using advanced skills of listening, questioning and observation or feedback. They are less likely to offer expert advice or guidance, as they are more committed to the other person's finding their own solutions.

While mentoring appears to be a more 'directive' activity, good mentors often have coaching skills, because without the ability to listen, question and offer challenge or feedback, a mentor's advice may be irrelevant or unwelcome.

When being directive 'works'

There's nothing wrong with being directive; in fact sometimes it's the best approach. Perhaps your colleague has no information or experience to draw upon in solving their issue. Maybe they need to know where to find a piece of data on the system, and it's pointless to ask them where they think they might find it. Or, sometimes, asking someone to think and decide for themselves is not possible: there may be a standard process they need to follow, to adhere to regulations. Sometimes, if someone is anxious or under pressure, asking them to decide something for themselves can make matters worse. Typically, when we are panicking we're less able to think clearly, and what we need is reassurance and guidance, rather than more pressure. Asking a series of challenging questions to someone who's anxious isn't going to help – although asking a question that helps them to calm down might!

 **brilliant** tip

Stop telling, start asking!

Coaching can be a quick and simple adjustment. For example, instead of your hearing about a problem and responding with, 'OK, here's what you need to do ...', simply ask your colleague, 'OK, what do you think needs to happen?'

When being directive works less well

Being consistently directive is an inflexible style that creates pitfalls for a manager over time. People who are always told what to do don't learn effectively, and potentially become bored, lacklustre or demotivated.

being consistently directive is an inflexible style that creates pitfalls

Since they are not encouraged to think, they may also become dependent or even lazy, asking their manager for frequent, or basic, instruction. Sometimes a person's sense of empowerment reduces as they become hesitant or lack the confidence to act. When they follow direct instructions, they might not be as engaged in their manager's solutions as they could be ('Well, I'll do it because you've told me to, but it's not going to work').

Another consequence of an overly directive manager is that subordinates aren't stimulated to think for themselves and so their own creativity or thinking processes are dulled. Solving problems becomes something the manager does, so why bother thinking about what the solutions might be?

OK, so where does being helpful fit in?

Ironically, while a manager may feel they are trying to help their team, they are actually creating a downward spiral. Managers find that more demands are made of them as they are called upon to direct situations and have all the answers (and inevitably sometimes they don't). This means that managers have less available time to focus on their own tasks, because all their time is taken up by the people who report to them. If only they could free up time, they could contribute more to their situations and exercise a higher level of involvement that a managing role demands: for example, supporting their own manager, or deciding priorities for the team as a whole.

Directive or self-directed – the consequence over time

As a manager, how you manage and influence affects both the nature of your relationship with your team and also how they develop over time.

Managers often complain that they want people working for them to act more proactively, yet the source of their dependency on the manager is often the manager themselves. With good intentions, managers sometimes 'help' or 'look after' the people who work for them, by offering clear instruction. When a manager is frequently directive, their relationship with a subordinate can feel like that of 'parent-to-child'. The manager 'parents' the subordinate, by giving detailed instructions and solutions instead of encouraging them to work things out for themselves. Over time, this 'parenting' means the subordinate feels dependent on the manager.

Figure 1.2 illustrates how the directive and self-directed styles impact relationships and responses over time.

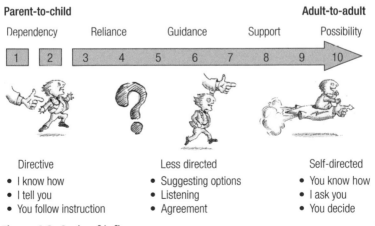

Figure 1.2 Scale of influence

When a manager encourages a subordinate to think, act and learn for themselves, the relationship feels more like 'adult-to-adult'. Over time, subordinates learn to expect being challenged by questions such as 'What are you suggesting?' or 'What's the real issue we need to solve here?' As they predict the manager's coaching response, they come prepared with opinions, ideas and suggestions more often. Over time, they'll feel an increased sense of engagement and ownership of their own situations as well.

 **questions**

How directive are you?

Use the following questions to assess how often you coach and how often you direct, or 'tell'. Maybe you'd also like to return to these questions once you've worked more with this subject, e.g. after you've finished this book.

Q How often do you give specific, direct instruction to people who work for you?

Q When people are explaining issues, challenges or difficulties, how much listening and questioning do you do – and how much talking?

Q How frequently do you offer specific ideas or advice to the people you work with?

Q If someone tells you about a problem, do *you* try to solve it?

Q Does it ever feel as though you are 'parenting' your team?

Based on your answers to the above, rate your own style of influence, using the 1–10 scale in Figure 1.2. Now get someone you know and trust to give their view of your typical style. Finally, look for opportunities to improve your scores, perhaps through discussion with the same person.

 **brilliant** recap

What is coaching?

We coach people by encouraging them to think and decide for themselves more often, and we do this by using heightened levels of skills such as listening, questioning, reflection and feedback. When managers coach people who work for them and with them, they aim to create a positive impact both on people's immediate performance and on their ongoing development. Coaching in the workplace is now a key skill for any manager, plus an effective tool of influence for anyone who engages in conversation with others.

CHAPTER 2

What is the mindset of a coaching manager?

n this chapter we'll look at the underlying values and beliefs that drive behaviour and management style. Hopefully you'll reflect on what you believe it means to be a manager, because knowing what kind of manager you currently are, or what kind of manager you'd like to be, can help you develop further. We'll look at traditional directive models of management as well as the values that underpin a coaching style of manager.

As you consider the idea of coaching, let's look at how you think you add value as a manager. If you believe 'My team value my experience and my ability to give them an expert opinion', then that's going to affect what you do. Or if you think that being a manager means helping your team to be successful, then your everyday actions will reflect that. When we decide to operate from different principles or develop new skills, we first need to know what our typical tendencies are, so we can change them. Because when we are self-aware, we have choice.

> when we are self-aware, we have choice

What beliefs might cause us to be a consistently directive manager?

Today's work environments often have multi-disciplined teams, with 'general managers' managing them. Unfortunately, we see the same managers feeling a pressure to 'know all the answers' or 'have the final word'. There is a subtle pressure that goes with being the most senior person in the team. And that pressure is that you know everything, or at least the 'right' thing. After all, they made you the boss, didn't they? Even where a manager does have all the answers, as we've described earlier, sometimes they add more value to their team by encouraging the team to find those answers on its own.

Let's look at what underlying assumptions a 'directive manager' might have and the behaviours that flow from those. Figure 2.1 illustrates what the values and beliefs of a constantly directive manager might be, and predicts skills and behaviours that result.

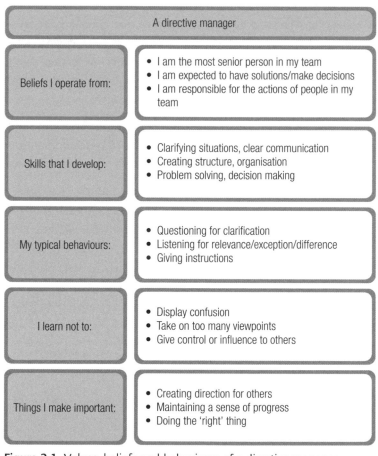

Figure 2.1 Values, beliefs and behaviours of a directive manager

This model is not bad or wrong; in fact there are times when this directive model creates strong leadership. Sometimes direction and instruction give confidence and clarity to others. In the armed forces a directive model suits many situations, including combat. Why, then, is the UK military now investigating coaching styles of leadership and considering their value in some situations? This is because, over time, the directive model exposes pitfalls, both in the relationships and in the results it creates. Here are some of those pitfalls.

● The manager puts themselves under pressure to know everything and 'be right' all the time.

● The team assume the manager wants to be involved and 'give answers', which takes more of the manager's time and can result in a 'fire-fighting' type of role for the manager.

● In their tendency to rely on the manager, the team appears lazy, demotivated or lacking in confidence, which causes frustration for the manager ('I sometimes feel like I'm nursemaid').

 brilliant definition

Facilitation

To facilitate a conversation is to help guide it through to a logical completion. A facilitator is focused more on the process of the conversation than the content of it: their role is to guide the group through the planned stages of the conversation. In a pure facilitation role, you will not contribute any content to the discussion yourself, you are simply there to encourage the group to work, keep the discussion relevant, close down or open up conversation, keep time, etc. Your priority is to make the session effective by supporting others to think for themselves.

What beliefs help us to be a coaching manager?

Managers who adopt a more consistently coaching style are operating from a different set of assumptions or beliefs. These beliefs enable them to relax some of the pressures to 'know everything' or to 'control and direct'. Coaching managers place value on people's ability to think and act for themselves, or on creating the conditions in which their own team will be successful. This will affect what their priorities are, on an everyday basis. For example, as a coaching manager you'll make sure that people have what they need to do a great job. That might be a shared vision, a sense of engagement, or just the knowledge and skills they need to create results. The basic start point might be 'What do they need to succeed?' rather than 'How do I make sure everyone's doing the right thing?' It may not appear to be a huge difference, but over time it shapes both attitude and approach. It's a little like altering the course of a ship by a few degrees: fairly quickly you end up somewhere completely different. Let's look at the values and beliefs of a coaching manager. Figure 2.2 illustrates these and predicts skills and behaviours that result.

> coaching managers place value on people's ability to think and act for themselves

If a manager believes that much of the value they add is to develop the people around them, then they will more naturally develop the skills of a coach. For example, in one-to-one meetings with individual team members, they are likely to offer feedback and challenge before advice and ideas. In team meetings, they will facilitate the discussion more than direct it, preferring to hear from the team members around the table. To a coaching manager, people's ability to think and act for themselves is more important than displaying their own knowledge.

A coaching manager	
Beliefs I operate from:	• Relationships with my team are based on equality • My subordinates can generate great solutions • My team are responsible for results they create
Skills that I develop:	• Focused listening, open questions, facilitation • Reflection, feedback, open observation • Empathy, relating to different character types
My typical behaviours:	• Seeking first to understand • Challenging interpretations, barriers or false limits • Encouraging others to think and act responsibly
I learn not to:	• Quickly offer solutions • Eagerly display how knowledgeable I am • Control the direction of conversations
Things I make important:	• Creating a context in which I can coach others • The learning and development of people • People's ability to think and act for themselves

Figure 2.2 Values, beliefs and behaviours of a coaching manager

Developing your own style

The purpose of offering these two models is not to prove either as right or wrong but simply to highlight the impact of a manager's self-image. Indeed, it's likely that you may blend the two styles in a way that works for you, and Chapter 7 (A flexible style of influence) is designed to help you do just that. But please don't allow a lack of ability to create a false limit upon you. By developing the flexibility to adopt either style, you can choose. When you have the skill to manage in both a directive and a non-directive way, you can adapt to situations and people to produce consistently good results.

 **questions**

What is important to you?

Use the following questions to assess your own style of management.

Q What are the core skills of an effective manager? What must they do well?

Q Do you see yourself as equal to your team? Or do you feel parental towards them?

Q How comfortable are you with making mistakes?

Q When people around you make mistakes, how do you typically react?

Q Reflecting on the two previous models (directive and coaching manager), which values and beliefs do you recognise as being most relevant to your own?

Q How does the pressure of a situation affect your ability to stay flexible, in terms of your management style?

Q What three things could you do more of, or less of, that would improve the effectiveness of your management style?

If you're comfortable, ask the opinion of someone you trust, to offer additional ideas or insights.

 **brilliant** recap

What is the mindset of a coaching manager?

Before you can develop the skills and behaviours of a coach in the workplace, first consider how you think you add value in your role. Our typical behaviours and responses are affected by what we think is important. If we want to be perceived as an 'expert' or 'helper', then coaching behaviours such as listening or questioning come less naturally. As an 'expert' or 'helper' we are more likely to develop a directive style of giving ideas, opinions and solutions. Once we have self-awareness of the beliefs or values that drive our behaviour, we can make the appropriate adjustments. This might be as simple as remembering that 'Their ability to think is more important than my "helping" by giving solutions'. When we focus on the beliefs of a coaching manager, we are more likely to interrupt our compulsion to be directive and become more able to coach people instead.

CHAPTER 3

How does our ego limit our ability to coach?

H ere we'll look at how one of the big barriers to coaching other people is our own sense of self (our ego). We'll look at the challenge of relaxing our natural urge to retain a sense of control during a conversation, e.g. to solve the problem or know the answer. We'll also learn how this compulsion runs much deeper than a learnt management style. By introducing the subject of the ego and how we relate to ourselves, we will touch upon questions and ideas that will help you to become more aware of your ego and the strength of influence it can have upon you in your work environment.

Ego – what ego?

Our ego is a function of our mind, like a built-in program that influences our thoughts and how we feel. Your ego suggests your sense of who you are and, perhaps more importantly, who you're not. If I ask you to describe yourself, or what it's like to be you, the descriptions you'll give me are likely to have been formed by your ego as it tried to make sense of being you, for example 'I'm a fireman, doctor, IT person, sales person, people person', etc. Knowing that you are a fireman, for instance, creates things that you are not, e.g. I'm not a sales person, etc. Similarly, other ideas you have about yourself might include 'I'm a conscientious worker, I'm an experienced

> your ego suggests your sense of who you are

manager, inexperienced manager'. Your ego has formed this part of your identity by comparing how you work to how others work. You also compare who you are with who you think other people are. In this way, the ego creates how it feels to be you in relation to the people and the world around you.

 'Your ego is a false identity that your mind constructed and then you took up residence in.'

Brandon Bays

Our ego begins to develop when we are a baby, as we naturally try to make sense of being conscious in our body. So we begin to notice where our body ends and the rest of the world begins. We have discovered a sense of our 'self' as being separate and different from everything else, and then our ego continues to adjust and develop over time. By the time you are an adult, you have a much more developed sense of who you are, and feelings of who you are not. Some of this is practical information and some of it creates behaviours that reinforce separateness from people and situations. For example, it's useful to have an idea of yourself as a 'good' person as it gives you some standards to judge your own behaviour against sometimes. Perhaps you'd stop yourself from saying or doing something unkind, simply because it didn't feel like 'you' to do that. But it's less useful when our ego perception of 'being a good person' develops further into 'righteousness' and places us in a position of being above judgement. Our ego can misinform us as well as inform us and, as Brandon Bays suggests, we use the way our ego perceives the world to create a 'false identity' that we become accustomed to living in and forget to question.

The common misrepresentation of the word 'ego'

Unfortunately, in common use the term 'ego' is used to describe an attribute of someone who appears arrogant or overconfident. We're all familiar with the saying, 'He's got a huge ego!' Actually, we all have an ego, but it's neither 'big' nor 'small' – it's just our ego. If we wanted to measure the ego, it's more useful to consider its strength rather than its size, i.e. how much influence does your ego have upon you? For example, could you purposely wear mismatching clothes that look really strange to other people or would your self-image stop you from being able to do that? Our ego can control us in different ways, some of which are the opposite of arrogance or overconfidence. For example, a person who describes themselves as 'painfully shy' still has a strong ego acting upon them. If they literally find it difficult to speak and express themselves in some circumstances, this is due to the controlling nature of their ego making them feel 'self-conscious'. When a shy person learns to relax this 'consciousness of self', e.g. by focusing less on themselves and more on other people, they will often find themselves more able to calm those feelings of shyness.

The most common mistake we make is to assume that the ego *is* who we are, rather than seeing it as a constructed idea of our self and how we 'ought' to behave. Part of how the ego works is to compare, contrast and judge, as a natural function of understanding itself in contrast to what is around it. So the ego is naturally geared to keep us separate; noticing what's the same, what's different, what we are in control of and what we are not in control of. People wanting to explore their own spirituality sometimes work to free themselves from the influence or ideas constructed by the ego. Doing this can bring a sense of freedom and liberation, for example an increased feeling of connection or relatedness to the world around us or a greater affinity to people. Instead of this 'spiritual enlightenment' we can also strive towards a simpler goal of 'everyday illumination'. By increasing our awareness of the key features and drives of our ego, we can create more self-awareness and choice in situations. (If you are interested in studying this whole topic in more depth, I would recommend *A New Earth* by Eckhart Tolle. In this book, Tolle provides a clearer sense of our own ego, and encourages us to work with that in practical, everyday situations.)

As we saw in the examples earlier, your sense of who you are often relates to the job role or title you've been given, for example 'I'm a junior manager/senior manager'. In reality, it's all false, as all those roles are invented, along with the boundaries or limitations they suggest. But in daily life we act as though the roles are real. Partly that's practical, as it helps to organise the work we do together. Defined roles also help people to play to their strengths, for example 'I'm a technical expert – that's what people expect'. For many people their sense of 'who they think they are' becomes a real driving force behind what they do or how they feel in everyday situations. For example, if the organisation has defined you as a junior manager, does that make you apprehensive about speaking to groups of senior managers? And perhaps more comfortable speaking to groups of lower-ranked staff? Or, if you're a senior manager, how does it affect your behaviour in a meeting with people you imagine are 'more junior'?

Now, keeping your personal image of being a manager in the office, imagine your holiday this year is a Caribbean cruise. Unfortunately the ship sinks. So you find yourself at sea, marooned on a life raft full of fellow tourists, like yourself. Then one of them explains they have extensive sailing and navigation skills. How does 'who you think you are' change during this experience? Maybe you stop thinking of yourself as a manager or tourist and start feeling like a victim – or a member of an amateur crew who needs to support the recently appointed skipper of the life raft. But is that new you true? Does who you are ever change? How can it?

 **questions**

How strong is your ego?

Use the following questions to become more aware of your own ego. They are in no way scientific – have fun recognising the forms in which your ego expresses itself!

Q How conscious are you of 'status' or 'position' – either your own or someone else's?

Q How good are you at being 'wrong'? For example, can you admit you are wrong? Can you apologise?

Q How much are you concerned by what other people think about you? Are you affected by their opinion or approval?

Q What effect does criticism have upon you?

Q How easily embarrassed are you?

Q How much do you resist being controlled by other people in situations?

Q How easily do you laugh at yourself?

Once again, if you're comfortable, perhaps ask someone whom you trust to offer additional views on your typical behaviour and tendencies.

The question of control

As human beings, we have a natural compulsion to maintain our sense of comfort or surety by being 'in control'. We like to maintain our sense of control in a number of ways, such as ensuring we know roughly what's going to happen in a situation, or even making something happen exactly the way we want it to. We work to control other people and situations, and we might do that by being directive, or more subtly manipulative, or even just by wishing something to happen. Because of the ego's driver to 'fix' things in position, our need to have surety, avoid change or maintain control is hugely influenced by our ego.

> we work to control other people and situations

Some of us behave in a more controlling way than others, and certain situations provoke us to be more controlling than others. For example, your colleague is preparing a report on the environmental policy of the company, which is a topic you're already frustrated about. You see opportunities to make a big difference with small changes and you don't feel anyone really cares about the whole issue. Your compulsion to control may range from needing to influence the report's recommendations, to having the headings set in a certain typeface. Or, less logically perhaps, you might withdraw from commenting on the report, but the idea that you're not involved may really annoy you. Your internal 'resistance' to what's happening is an indication that you want things to be a different way and the emotions that arise from your need to control can confuse your behavioural responses. For example, in the environmental report situation, you may get so annoyed about the situation that you end up saying nothing – which seems a contradiction!

 questions

How do you seek to control?

This compulsion to control our world may or may not be an obvious thing to us, so the following exercise might help. Use the questions to assess your own compulsions to control. Again, they are in no way scientific – they're simply intended to provoke further thought.

- Ⓠ How 'opinionated' are you; for example, how strong are your opinions about certain things?
- Ⓠ How much advice do you give to other people?
- Ⓠ How do you behave (or feel) if you don't get your own way?
- Ⓠ How much do you control yourself in situations, e.g. 'I would never do that'.
- Ⓠ How well do you respond to unexpected change? For example, the big meeting's cancelled, your flight's cancelled, the hotel is double-booked, or the school isn't going to take your children after all.
- Ⓠ How much do you notice feeling 'controlled' by other people and situations? For example, do you get annoyed if you feel someone is dominating you?
- Ⓠ If you give someone good advice and they completely ignore it, how do you feel?

Once again, if you're comfortable, perhaps ask someone whom you trust to offer additional views on your typical behaviour and tendencies.

How does our ego affect us in coaching?

You ego is a powerful influence on you and one that you need to be aware of if you are to develop free choice of your responses in coaching situations. By 'free choice' I mean choices that aren't limited by who you think you are or who others think you are (or are not). In coaching we sometimes make responses based on our self-image and we don't know we're doing that. Our idea of who we think we are, and so what's 'normal' for us, creates a limit on our thought and choices. It's a little like saying, 'I can't give all this up to go and study the polar ice caps – I'm a finance director for goodness sake.' If that person felt they had pure choice in their life, the career change would be a valid option to consider.

When you recognise how your current self-image in the workplace affects your thoughts and behaviour in a coaching conversation, you can relax those 'auto-responses' more often. For example, if you have the self-concept of 'the manager', can you still listen to someone criticise the company without being defensive? If you are to be an effective coach, you need to be able to do that.

Relate to someone else's world, by relaxing your grip on yours

As a coach, the influence of our opinions or values must be reduced in a coaching conversation. That's because to relate effectively to the person we are coaching, we must do so on their terms, and in their 'world'. Imagine you're coaching a teenager on the topic of taking drugs: does giving them your strong (adult) views on that help? Or does it work better to relate to what it's like for a teenager growing up and to use that as a start point? This is an extreme example, but the principle of 'standing in someone else's shoes' is a key tool of influence, and if you're too attached to your own viewpoint you may find that difficult.

> to relate effectively to the person we are coaching, we must do so on their terms

 **brilliant** tip

Notice your ego through your emotions

Noticing your ego and its compulsions is the first step towards reducing its ability to affect you. You can often spot signs of your ego's control over you through the emotions you suddenly feel. For example, negative emotions may be brought on by something as simple as an unexpected delay or change of plans. Feelings of stress or frustration about something are often triggered by a sense of being 'out of control'. Learn to focus on feelings of *acceptance* of how things are, and relax the grip of your ego upon you.

The irrelevance of right and wrong

The ego has a fixed viewpoint, for example ideas of what's 'right' and what's 'wrong', or an attachment to how things 'should' be. If your ego is a strong influence on you, you'll have urges to operate from these ideas of 'right' and 'wrong' continually. I'm not talking about large-scale views here, such as 'it's bad to kill people'; I'm referring to less clear issues, such as whether we should be made to recycle, or if it's wrong to park in reserved parking spaces. As a coaching example, maybe your coachee criticises someone you know and like. As a coach you need to stay with their views, exploring them, reflecting them and challenging them only as part of the conversation. It doesn't work if you automatically leap to that person's defence. Maybe they've said that Sally is a liar and a cheat and you don't agree with that. You now have options.

1 *Disagree with the view and state a contradicting opinion.* This is likely to create a sense of disagreement and potentially reduce rapport as the coachee is made to defend or justify their view. It may also distract the conversation on to a topic

that's actually irrelevant to the conversation, for example Sally (and your views of her). The conversation may best be centred on what's caused the coachee's remarks, i.e. their response to Sally or how they've got this view.

2 *Ignore your disagreement and act as if you agree.* Possibly a worse option than the first, as you've traded integrity for an attempt to please the coachee, or at least avoid breaking rapport with them. This may actually be done quite subtly, for example 'Yes, I can see what you're saying' or 'Yes, I guess I can imagine her doing that'. If actually neither of those statements is true (because you can't see what they're saying, or imagine Sally doing that) then that constitutes a lie – so your integrity is corrupted.

3 *Stay in a neutral posture and don't react to the critical nature of the remark.* This is the more effective option, as it retains rapport and integrity. Also, as you ignore your own desire to defend Sally, you retain an objective, impartial view of the coachee's remarks. For example, you are able to see beyond what that person is saying, and stay interested in why they might say that. But by offering them neutral territory in which to consider their views, you help them to relax and become a little more objective. As you ask them about their accusations, they explain themselves, and as they do they realise that their view is a bit extreme. By listening and questioning further, you've loosened or relaxed that person's views.

I'm not saying that as a coach you need to ignore your own views, judgements and values, but by staying detached from your own opinions you can keep to the purpose of the conversation, which is to have someone think for themselves. When we coach someone, the conversation aims to elicit someone else's thoughts, and that requires a stronger focus on them. By appreciating the influence of your own ego in a conversation, you can work to create that stronger focus.

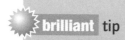 **brilliant** tip

You won't beat your ego by fighting with it

The best way to reduce the influence of your own ego is to notice it, acknowledge it and create a sense of detachment from it. By detachment I mean to recognise that your ego isn't you, it's simply a function of your mind. Resisting your ego, for instance by getting frustrated with yourself when symptoms of it arise, won't help. Simply notice its signs (such as a desire to control or having rules about needing things to be a certain way), acknowledge them, and then choose consciously what your response to a situation will be.

How might our ego affect our learning?

To create a sense of freedom around your development as a coach, you need to relax ideas of who you think you are now. Perhaps you think you'll never be a good coach because you're too domineering? Or because you lack confidence? Or because you 'know too much'? Having an idea of 'who you are now' fixes a start point for your journey, which again may be a false limit. You might imagine the journey to be longer than it needs to be, or the terrain ahead a little rocky. And after all, why would you want to put limits on the adventure of learning?

brilliant tip

How do I know my ego is *less* strong?

It's possible that you don't have a very strong ego – see how many of the following indicators apply to you.

● You're able to take direct criticism well.

● You're relaxed about being proved wrong in a situation.

● You can laugh at yourself easily.

- You cope with unexpected change well, for example you stay resourceful in a crisis.

- You don't get 'hung up' on what other people think about you.

- You're relaxed about issues of status or position.

- You're able to accept people with very different views from your own.

- You're not easily embarrassed.

- You can accept how things are, even when they're not how you want them to be.

- You feel little need to impress, control or 'please' people in situations; instead you navigate by your own personal sense of what's right and wrong.

Maybe some of these are true of you and some aren't. Whatever the case, all of us have opportunities to develop further, so I encourage you to reflect on your own strength of ego.

Going beyond ego

Good coaches (and managers) have learnt to reduce the influence of their ego upon them. This is because they have relaxed limits on their thinking and some of the automatic responses that are driven by their ego. For example, if the subordinate they are coaching begins to criticise a decision that they (as manager) have made, they are not automatically compelled to defend or justify that decision, or perhaps take control of the conversation. Instead they

> good coaches have learnt to reduce the influence of their ego

are able to remain in a more neutral posture, and stay aware of what the subordinate is saying. After all, the most important thing may not be the issue of whether or not the decision is a good one, but more that the subordinate is anxious about it and needs to deal with that.

As an incentive, some of the benefits of learning to relax the influence of your ego in coaching conversations include:

- less stress, e.g. from seeking to be in control, or resisting what you perceive as being controlled by others
- increased energy and sense of being 'freed up', e.g. from who you are and who you are not
- increased sense of 'possibility' in situations, e.g. constantly working to control takes effort and creates a false limit on what happens (or what you allow to happen)
- increased sense of flexibility and 'easy-goingness', i.e. by your decreased sense of attachment to how things are, or how they should be
- increased openness, trust and relatedness to others as you become more 'real' to them (rather than the image of yourself that you work to project).

 **brilliant** recap

How does our ego limit our ability to coach?

Our sense of self (our ego), or who we think we are, can impair our ability to coach other people. That's because our idea of who we are brings with it a raft of assumptions and beliefs, about what's important and what's not. For example, if we identify strongly with the role of manager, that often dictates certain rules of behaviour, based on our beliefs about that position. Those rules of behaviour may prevent us from adopting some of the core principles of coaching, such as equality, openness or a need to relate to someone else in their world. By recognising the influence of our own ego upon us in situations, we can develop more 'pure choice' in situations. This enables us to stay flexible around the people we are coaching, and more present to their views and feelings.

PART 2

Ability

T his part of the book looks at the basic skills of coaching for managers and offers ideas for how you might develop those further. We will focus on just the core skills, as these will help you the most as you coach in your workplacc. The core skills of management coaching are:

Build rapport
or relationship

Constructive
feedback

Focused
listening

Flexible
style of influence

Effective
questioning

There are obviously other skills that are useful, such as the ability to observe non-verbal communication, but it's best to begin with the basics, and lay a firm foundation on which to build. Please remember that you already have some ability in all five skills. Maybe you're already an effective listener, or maybe you promote warmth and trust easily. The aim is to help you develop in these areas, for example by understanding why sometimes you don't listen as well.

CHAPTER 4

Building rapport or relationship

Build rapport
or relationship

Constructive feedback

Focused listening

Flexible style of influence

Effective questioning

This chapter will explain what rapport is, and why it's relevant in coaching. We'll look at the features and causes of good and poor rapport, so you'll know what affects it. You'll also be encouraged to think about how *you* experience rapport, and how you might develop this important coaching skill further.

What is rapport?

Rapport is the skill of building a relationship, either in a brief moment, like a quick conversation, or over time in a longer-term relationship. Rapport refers to your quality of relatedness or relationship to someone else. That might be relatedness in the present moment, for example 'I'm feeling comfortable with this person', or it might refer to a relationship over time, for example 'I always enjoy talking to her'.

You may experience good rapport as feelings of warmth, comfort or 'sameness'. The rapport between you and another person will affect both you and them. For example, when you have good rapport you are likely to feel comfortable and be able to 'be yourself', i.e. act naturally. The other person is also likely

two people with good rapport are more likely to trust each other to experience similar feelings as they too experience this sense of comfort. Two people with good rapport are also more likely to trust each other, and their willingness to be open with each other will increase.

Poor rapport might be experienced as 'coolness' or a sense of being different from another person. This feeling of being 'different' from someone else might also create feelings of separateness or detachment. That may or may not be an issue, depending on your objectives in the situation.

A scale of rapport

There is a common misunderstanding that we either 'have' or 'don't have' rapport in a situation. This is unhelpful because it suggests that we either do or don't have a relationship with someone. But where we are relating in any way to another person – for example in conversation, via email, on the telephone – then we are connecting to them. This connection is a relationship of some sort, which is rapport. Whether that relationship is warm or cool is simply an indicator of the quality of that rapport. It's as if there are levels of rapport, or a scale that moves above and below a neutral position. Figure 4.1 illustrates this idea of levels of rapport.

Why is rapport so important?

One reason why rapport is needed in coaching is that you need good rapport if you want to influence someone constructively, i.e. without dictating to them. Because we're giving fewer directives, we can't just 'tell' someone to do something – so we need good rapport. Also, when we coach, we encourage people to think for themselves, and that 'encouraging' is much harder without good rapport. Rapport creates a climate of openness and trust and helps people express

> rapport creates a climate of openness and helps people express themselves naturally

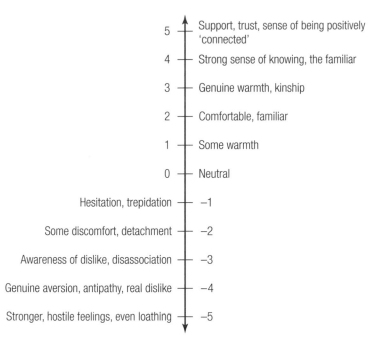

Figure 4.1 Scale of rapport

themselves naturally. Plus, we sometimes need to challenge people or give them feedback in a way that builds confidence rather than discomfort. To be heard effectively – as a supportive colleague rather than as an enemy – we need good rapport.

What affects rapport?

Rapport is built on features of sameness. Basically, where we feel we are the same as someone else, we feel more connection to them than if we think we are different. These features of sameness can include:

- how we appear physically, for example appearance, clothing, racial background, etc.

- how we speak, for example qualities of voice, energy, volume, speed

- what words we use, for example same jargon, key phrases
- the sameness or difference of our 'body language', for example I use lots of hand gestures and so do you
- the values or beliefs we seem to have, for example you're a vegetarian and so am I, or you support a certain football team, etc.

The above list is as relevant for boardrooms in business as it is for gang culture on the streets. When you look like me, sound like me, seem like me then I'll feel more comfortable with you. Try going to work in your gardening clothes and see the difference in how people respond to you (unless you work in a garden centre, of course). And if someone's accent or manner is very different from yours, does it take you a little longer to establish rapport? In the workplace or on the streets, we all have our buzzwords, common language or acronyms that distinguish us.

 **exercise**

Go and watch rapport in action

Choose a situation where groups of people are present. Watch and listen for a while, then ask yourself the following questions.

- How do you know if people are 'getting along well'? Look for physical, vocal and energetic matching, for example are they as animated as each other?
- What are the signs that people are cool or detached towards each other? Look for signs of mismatching.
- What impact does good rapport have on a conversation or in a meeting?
- How does 'detachment' or lack of rapport impact the quality of a conversation?
- How does the quality of rapport in work relationships affect collaboration and results?

Use what you notice to reflect upon your own ability to build rapport with others.

How to build rapport

When you have good rapport with someone, you'll probably know. For example, you'll feel generally comfortable, and notice that they appear comfortable too. Understanding what impacts rapport is most valuable when you notice you haven't got it. Where rapport is not an issue, then I'd suggest you reduce your focus on it and even forget about it. But where you feel less comfortable and are aware that there's an issue with rapport in a situation, then you'll want to attend to that.

Let's assume that for most relationships in the workplace you need to be in the positive ranges on our scale of rapport. Here are some indications of rapport dipping into the negative ranges of rapport.

● You have a sense of separation, detachment, or 'difference'.

● You're feeling less comfortable in the conversation, i.e. you're not being 'natural'.

● You seem less able to express yourself or your ideas in a way that is understood.

● The other person seems lacking in warmth or openness towards you.

● The quality of mutual understanding is below what it needs to be.

The basic process you need to follow includes the following steps.

1 Relax! That's really important if you are going to be able to notice subtle signals, because if you're stressed or frustrated it's more difficult to be aware.

2 Next, have the intention to be more 'related' to the other person. For example, focus on a thought like 'How are we the same here?'

3 Notice what might be causing lack of rapport – look for major differences. Consider mismatches such as energy, body language or voice quality.

If you're fairly relaxed, have the intention to be related and then look for what's causing a lack of rapport, you're very likely to notice something useful. Once you have that idea, you can adapt your own behaviour in a natural way. For example, maybe you notice you've been doing most of the talking, or maybe the other person speaks with more, or less, energy than you do. Maybe the difference is what you both think about the situation (there's a lack of mutual understanding). You might choose to pull the conversation back to the start point, for example 'OK, let's confirm what we're both saying here, can you explain your view again?' When a person feels that you are genuinely listening to them, they are more likely to listen to you and your views. When mutual understanding is achieved, you can build on that.

 **questions**

Warm or cool – what's the difference?

Use the following questions to work with rapport principles for yourself.

1   Think of someone in a work situation with whom you feel you have *good* rapport, then ask yourself:

   Ⓠ How do you feel when you're with them?

   Ⓠ How do your feelings of good rapport with this person affect how you are when you're with them?

   Ⓠ How does this person seem the same as or similar to you?

2   Now think of someone in a work situation with whom you *don't* have good rapport. Try to choose someone with whom you want better rapport (rather than someone you simply don't like). Now reflect upon the following questions:

   Ⓠ How do you feel when you're with this person, for example talking to them?

   Ⓠ How do your feelings of poor rapport affect how you are when you're with them? For example, how natural are you?

> ⓠ How does this person seem different from or not the same as you?

3 Finally, with the person with whom you don't have good rapport, consider:

> ⓠ How would it benefit you to have better rapport with this person? For example, how would things be different?
>
> ⓠ How do your thoughts or feelings of 'difference' affect you around this person?
>
> ⓠ How can you encourage feelings of sameness or relatedness? For example, asking 'What do we have in common here?'

Your intention often makes the biggest difference. So have the intention to gain rapport, hold the thought for a while, then let it go. Also by focusing less on difference, and more on *how you are alike*, we build rapport more easily. Your 'being alike' may encompass many different things, from gestures to values or a sense of what's important.

Empathy creates relatedness, which creates connection

Empathy is the ability to relate to another person in their own terms and will help you to build rapport. Empathy requires that we notice another person's experience and sometimes how they're feeling. It can be as simple as saying 'I can see this might be frustrating for you'. When we

when we notice and acknowledge, we create feelings of relatedness

notice and acknowledge, we create feelings of relatedness. For example, you might complain that your current workload is resulting in your working long hours. If I hear that and don't acknowledge that in some way, you may feel that I am not relating to your situation appropriately. It may just take a simple remark like, 'OK, that's not great for you is it? Let's look at what's causing that.' But if I'd simply said 'Let's look at what's causing that', I might seem more detached from your situation.

 **brilliant** tip

Rapport – fast first principles

Let's say you've got an important conversation coming up and you want to be sure you build rapport quickly. What's something simple you can do?

● Make sure you're feeling calm, for example it often helps to breathe slowly from your stomach.

● Make sure that your attention is focused on the present, for example noticing what's happening in the present moment.

● Turn your attention to the person you want to establish rapport with, and notice key aspects of their style. For example, how much energy do they display? How quickly or loudly do they talk? What's their physical posture – closed, open, etc.?

● Use your intention to help you build rapport. For example, think 'How can I stay related to you?' and let this thought help you 'tune into' the other person and their world.

● Trust your ability to notice what you need to notice and, as you do so, make any adjustments necessary. For example, quieten your voice, or smile a little more, or slow down as you speak.

First try these ideas somewhere where the stakes are lower, for example with a person serving you in a shop, or in casual conversation. Notice the things that seem to make the most difference for you, such as the idea of 'tuning in' or matching energy.

 **brilliant** recap

Building rapport or relationship

If you want to encourage others to think and act for themselves, you must be able to create healthy levels of rapport. Rapport is built on features of sameness, and poor rapport normally indicates feelings of detachment or difference. By increasing your ability to relate to others on their own terms, you improve your ability for rapport and therefore influence.

CHAPTER 5

Focused
listening

N ow let's look at what we mean by focused listening, and what the features of good listening are. This chapter talks about what it takes to really listen to someone else and what sometimes gets in the way of that. You'll also find ways of practising listening to increase your normal capacity to listen.

In a coaching conversation, your requirement to listen goes beyond a simple need to hear information. When we do not listen well, our understanding of someone and their conversation reduces, as does our ability to react appropriately. Yet when we listen to someone really well, we can actually help them to speak and express themselves. It's as if they recognise they are really being listened to, and so can relax and simply speak (and if you've ever been partially ignored as you tried to explain something, you'll already know this). Great listeners often build rapport and warmth naturally, as they have an increased focus on other people.

Listening begins with intention and concentration

Good listening demands that we make a conscious effort to listen. Intention to listen is the beginning of that. A clear mind,

good listening demands that we make a conscious effort to listen

free of chatter is also needed – and that flows more easily from that initial intention. Listening is linked directly to our attention. When we're with someone and 'kind of' listening (but not really), our attention is partly on the person we are with and partly on our own thoughts. I call this 'cosmetic listening', as it has a superficial or cosmetic quality to it. While this quality of listening may be fine sometimes, for example when listening to the chatter of a child, it is ineffective within a coaching conversation. Poor concentration, being distracted and generally not making the other person important are all basic barriers that must be constantly overcome if you are going to be a strong listener. Developing a strong intention, clear focus and concentration will help you with that.

Staying present to people

The basic principle of good listening is actually that we need to 'be with' the person we are supposed to be listening to. This requires a sole focus upon them. What stops our focus and attention being on another person is a combination of internal and external distractions. Internal distractions may be our own thoughts, worries or 'mind chatter'. External distractions range from mobile phones to traffic noise to the weather – or indeed anything we allow our attention to rest on. One feature of our modern work culture is mobile communications and their tendency to interrupt person-to-person conversation. Sometimes 'real-person-to-real-person' conversations are made less important than the need to answer a phone when it rings, or check a mobile device when an email or text arrives. It's not as though we intend to make the person with us less important than the incoming call or message – but that can appear to be the underlying suggestion. If we are truly to listen to the person we are with, we must practise 'present-moment awareness' – this means we must clear our mind and focus on what's happening right now.

 **exercise**

Present-moment awareness

This exercise is valuable as a way of 'being present' both to yourself and to other people. If you know you tend to 'live in your mind', it's a good way of grounding you back into reality. It's also a way of reducing stress, or simply learning to appreciate what's happening around you. Use this anywhere (and everywhere) to practise being present.

● *Notice your surroundings.* Begin to notice your immediate surroundings in more detail, by turning your attention to them. What can you see around you? Look at things afresh, notice some detail, register where you are and what's happening (or not happening).

● *Notice your body.* Now notice your body – how it feels in its current position and posture. Alter that, if you want to, and accept how your body wants to align itself to your surroundings. Notice how your body feels, perhaps move a little more, and get a stronger sense of being in your body.

● *Notice your mind.* Next, notice your mind and what's going on with that. What thoughts are there? Knowing those thoughts are not needed right now, simply refocus on being in your body, in the environment you're in right now. Clear your mind by focusing only on what's happening now. If any thoughts drift in, simply notice them and refocus on what's happening now.

Filtered listening

Just as important as our effort to listen is our intention of *how* we are going to listen. For example, if I listen to you as someone who doesn't know very much, then that simple presupposition impacts upon what I hear. My assumption that 'you don't know very much' will cause me to filter what you say for things that confirm my belief. Alternatively, if I intend to listen to you as someone who has great knowledge, then the manner of my listening is changed. Think about sitting down with someone like Bill Clinton and asking him what he thinks about our environmental issues. How would your 'listening' be different if you asked the same question of your next-door neighbour? It might or might not be different, depending on how your beliefs about those people affect your 'listening' for them. Pearls of wisdom spoken by your next-door neighbour may not have as profound an impact upon you as the same ideas spoken by a statesman. That's why subjective qualities such as charisma or reputation are so highly prized in roles where influence is key to success. They have a marked effect on someone's ability to convince or persuade, as they create positive filters for an audience's listening.

Listening from nothing

A very different posture to adopt when you're with someone is to listen to them 'from nothing'. That is, having no presupposition of them, or what they are saying. As you listen to them, you experience them simply as they are in that moment, and focus on what they are saying – in that moment. Your mind is free of judgemental thoughts based on previous experiences of them, as though you are listening to them 'afresh'. When we listen to someone in this way, we experience the sensation of being 'present' to them. We have a sense of being with them, rather than being in our own mind, with our own thoughts. When you are listening to someone in this way, your mind is mostly still and quiet, as your focus is on what the other person is saying.

> focus on what they are saying – in that moment

 **brilliant** exercise

How do you listen?

Listening 'from nothing' is a challenge, as we need to clear our minds of what we already think about a person, based on our experience of them. Even if we've only just met someone, we form quick opinions or judgements about who we think they are, and what we think they are like. The following exercise is designed to help.

Think about a very recent conversation (or do this exercise after your next conversation). Then ask yourself:

● While the other person was talking, how much of your focus (or attention) was on what they were saying and how much was it on what you were thinking?

● How busy (or quiet) was your mind during the conversation?

● Were there any persistent thoughts or feelings you were having during the conversation? If there were, how did those thoughts affect you in the conversation?

● If we asked the other person to describe how 'listened to' they felt during that conversation, what do you think they would say?

● What would it take for you to be a better listener?

Use your responses to change your approach in a future conversation, perhaps even the next one! Try listening to someone in a different way and see if you can improve the quality of your listening.

Barriers to listening

None of us intends to be a poor listener, it's just that the barriers to listening are many and varied. Sometimes our attention is on ourselves and what we are thinking, rather than on the other person. For example, our mind may be full of our own thoughts or ideas. Or we subtly control the direction of the conversation, maybe to talk about things we know about, or things that are important to us. For example, you may think, 'All this talk about staff training is fine but I'm more interested in the real reason they're not getting things done.'

Another natural, human tendency is to want to put something of 'ourselves' into the conversation, perhaps to impress the other person or make them like us. For example, you might say 'Aha, I've had a similar situation in my area, let me tell you about it ...' Talking about our own experiences doesn't make us bad people – we are unlikely to have intended to distract the conversation from the speaker. But this example of poor self-awareness, i.e. not realising we are 'hijacking' the conversation, will reduce the quality of our listening. If I don't realise I'm telling the story about the 'similar situation in my area' simply to put 'me' into the conversation, then I'm unlikely to stop myself doing that. But when I recognise that it's an irrelevant piece of information, which will actually distract from the importance of what the other person is describing (the situation in *their* area), I can ignore my own urge to interrupt.

> poor self-awareness will reduce the quality of our listening

brilliant recap

Focused listening

For any manager and coach, focused listening is a valuable skill to develop. Effective listening allows us to tap into a rich seam of understanding and influence. When we listen properly to someone, we can literally increase their ability to express themselves. What stops us from listening in any situation is simply ourselves. Either we are distracted by our own thoughts or ideas, or we simply don't make the effort to focus on someone else. Really good listening demands that we make the other person more important in the conversation and 'let go' of the importance of ourselves. As we really focus on someone else with the intention of listening fully to them, the sense of ourselves, our ego, diminishes.

CHAPTER 6

Effective questioning

Build rapport
or relationship

Constructive
feedback

Focused
listening

Flexible
style of influence

**Effective
questioning**

I n this chapter, we will look at the principles of effective questioning, and the dos and don'ts of this important coaching skill. I'll offer examples of questions you might use more often, plus some with a specific purpose, for example to broaden a debate, shift someone's perspective or gather more specific information. You'll also find an exercise to help you start to ask better questions right away.

Great questions: a neat trick

People who ask quality questions generally obtain better quality answers. Have you ever sat in a meeting where someone has asked a really great question about a situation? Perhaps the conversation had become disjointed, or difficult to comprehend. Or maybe people seemed to have very different views and agreement seemed unlikely. Then someone asked a really great question. What effect did it have on the group? Perhaps it had a profound influence on a situation, perhaps by crystallising debate, or addressing the heart of a matter. Or perhaps it just brought things back on track. Asking a great question is often of much greater value than offering an idea or an opinion. And yet in a work context we often put more effort into forming ideas or opinions and explaining things from our perspective than asking great questions.

In coaching, a well-timed, perfectly worded question can turn keys, unlock doors and provoke insight for the person you're coaching. For example, 'If you could change just one thing about this situation, what would that be?' or 'What's really important to do first?' As the benefits of coaching rest upon our ability to have others think for themselves, then the quality of our questions becomes the oil for this mechanism.

> a well-timed, perfectly worded question can unlock doors

What are the attributes of a quality question? Generally, a quality question:

- is simple
- has a clear sense of purpose
- influences thought or learning – without being controlling.

brilliant tip

Coach the person not the issue

Remember that your focus during a coaching conversation is to help the person fix the issue – not for you to fix the issue. So ask questions that help *them* think about the situation, rather than help *you* think about the situation!

The power of keeping things simple

Great questions are not complicated; they are simple in their construction. If someone has to struggle to understand a question before they can attempt to answer it, we risk wasting energy and confusing someone's focus. For example, try answering the following question.

Considering the current nature of our world and our organisations as forming part of that world, what are the key obstacles that seem to pose the greatest prevailing threats upon the ability of organisations to contribute constructively to our environmental issues?

How did you like that? It took me right back to school exam papers! The question is long, complicated and seems to be 'getting at something', i.e. that there is a 'right' or 'wrong' response. It's fairly off-putting in its tone, and extreme just to prove a point. Let's simplify it a little and see how it changes the impact it has upon us.

What are the key obstacles that pose the greatest threats to the ability of organisations to contribute constructively to our environmental issues?

It's better for stripping away the pointless words, but we still have to work to comprehend its meaning, before we can use mental energy in forming our response. Words such as 'key obstacles' and 'constructively' seem significant – even though their meaning is unclear. Again, the question feels a little highbrow or 'exclusive'. Let's try another level of simplification.

What barriers do organisations face when trying to help with our environmental issues?

This question feels different, doesn't it? Now we can focus our energy on surfacing our response, rather than trying to understand what the question is asking us to do. This example is also more encouraging of an answer, as it has no 'cleverness' built into it. It is less intimidating or pressured – almost as though anyone can have a valid opinion. So simplifying language, using shorter words and terms, are all helpful when we want to be effective with our questions.

The following table offers further examples of the effects of simple and complicated questions.

Complicated question	Simpler version
What are the various issues or complications that have led us to where we are with this situation?	What's caused this?
Considering the after-effects of such an action, what are the consequences of such a move, do you think?	How will doing that affect things?
What kind of opinions or views might Bob bring to the table, do you think?	What does Bob think about this?

And if those sound really obvious, don't be fooled! Try listening to people in meetings or professional discussions and focus on the questions people use. Here are some of the reasons we use overly complex questions in a work situation.

- We like to appear smart, clever and knowledgeable – and asking 'What does Bob think?' might make us look slow. So we overcomplicate a thought or question, feeling that the simplest version of that may appear dumb. It may save time, focus the debate and provide a useful shift in perspective – but we don't get to sound 'clever', which may be a stronger urge.

- We start talking before we have a clear thought of what our question is. Our urge to talk, to be part of a conversation, may encourage us to begin a statement before we actually know where we are going with it. Clear questions demand clarity of mind and thought – sometimes we need to work on maintaining a relaxed yet focused state of mind first.

- We don't ask what we really want to know! Instead of asking a direct question, we 'strategise' around it. For example, we are listening and becoming confused as someone explains what a problem is. We are confused because it seems as though the problem has 'changed' during the conversation.

The dialogue below demonstrates these points.

Jayne   I'm fed up with the way Finance think that they can just change the way things are going to get done and then expect everyone else just to fall in line with whatever new piece of documentation they've invented. It's ridiculous.

Manager   Why? What documentation's changed?

Jayne   No, they haven't changed anything, it's just that they've implied that they might do. Moira in particular is really worried now.

Manager   [thinks] *I'm a bit confused ... what's the issue here?* [asks] Why is Moira worried?

Jayne   Well, because she's the one who's going to have to cope with the new documentation.

Manager   I thought there wasn't any new documentation?

 **exercise**

Go ask some questions . . .

Next time someone starts telling you about a problem (or starts complaining), try asking some or all of the following questions.

● What else/who else is affected by this?

● What's the real cause of this, do you think?

● What needs to happen then?

● What options are you considering?

● So what have you decided to do?

As you can see, each question has a different purpose. Individually, each question may be productive, and together they create a sense of forward movement, i.e. towards solution and action.

Although the manager becomes confused they may be reluctant to admit that. So they keep asking questions and hope they'll eventually get clear. They might get clear – or they might not. It's quite likely they'll waste time pursuing different lines of enquiry (like 'What documentation "might" be changing?'). Here's how asking the question that first occurred to them affects things.

Jayne   I'm fed up with the way Finance think that they can just change the way things are going to get done and then expect everyone else just to fall in line with whatever new piece of documentation they've invented. It's ridiculous.

Manager Why? What documentation's changed?

Jayne   No, they haven't changed anything, it's just that they've implied that they might do. Moira in particular is really worried now.

Manager [thinks] *I'm a bit confused … what's the issue here?* [asks] So, Jayne, I'm a bit confused, what's the issue here?

Jayne   Well, just their complete lack of consultation with us, they're just not keeping us in the loop.

Again, it's a simple example to prove a point. When we ask what's really on our minds, rather than rewording it, or translating it into something slightly different, we retain the integrity of our first impulse. Our first impulse is often the clearest thought we have, and the one that can create the greatest clarity in a situation. It's often a simple thought – and so 'not very clever' and less appealing to us as a question we want to voice publicly.

When clever isn't clever . . .

Our tendency to value simplicity more lowly than apparently 'intelligent' debate will stop us asking effective questions. Have you ever sat in a meeting feeling really confused about the discussion and stayed quiet? Then someone else voiced their own confusion, asked for clarification and it was useful to everyone? The conversation had become confused or irrelevant and yet most of the group had avoided asking for clarification. A simple question was all that was needed to pull things back on track. Simple questions borne from a clear intention create effective progress, especially in coaching conversations.

> simple questions borne
> from a clear intention
> create effective progress

 **brilliant** exercise

What's in a question?

The following exercise is intended to help you become more aware of the types of questions you typically hear – and also those that you yourself ask.

Pick a conversation where people are discussing something as a group. If you are part of that group, you can also consider your own contributions afterwards. Listen to the types of questions that are being asked, and reflect on the following questions.

● How often are people asking questions, and how often are they simply responding to what has been said?

● What impact does a lack of questions have?

● When people do ask questions, how effective are they, i.e. what impact do those questions have on the discussion?

● Which types of questions work well – and which don't?

● If you asked questions, what was your intention or purpose behind those questions?

Take a little time to consider how you might improve the quality (and impact) of your own questions, having observed the behaviours of yourself and others.

Questions with a clear sense of purpose

Another attribute of an effective question is that it has a clear purpose or objective. For example, that purpose may be to gather more information, to encourage ideas, or to motivate someone to act. When we don't have a clear sense of purpose behind our question, the question will often be confused or get a result that we didn't want. In coaching, this is important because we want our questions to help the other person progress in some way. The following table of questions illustrates questions with clear purpose. They are also nice, simple questions you might use in your everyday work situations.

Purpose	Coaching examples
Gather general information	Can you say more about that?
Gather specific information	Specifically, what is it that you're unhappy about? Can you tell me what actually happened?
Help someone remember something more clearly	What else can you remember?
To refocus someone on what's important, for example keep them on track, or calm them down	OK, so what's really important about all this? What seems to be the most important thing for us to focus on now?
Understand someone's values	What is important to you about that? Why is that important to you?
Help someone appreciate another person's perspective	What might be Jody's reasons behind asking for this? What's important to Jody? If we had Jody here, how would she describe this situation?
Get someone to link two thoughts, or situations, together	How do your work pressures relate to what you said about developing the team more?

Purpose	Coaching examples
Help someone come to a conclusion	What are your thoughts about this now? What is the conclusion you are drawing from this now?
Produce ideas without a sense of pressure	What options are there? What options are available to you? What things might you do? What ideas are you having?
Influence someone to decide	Which option do you prefer? What have you decided to do?
Influence someone to action	What could you do about that right now?
Prepare someone to overcome barriers to taking action	What might stop you from doing that? [*Follow-up*] So how will you overcome that?

 **brilliant** tip

Is this a closed question?

If you're going to be an effective coach you'll want to develop an ability to ask consistently open questions, i.e. questions that cannot be answered with a yes or a no. To remind you, open questions begin with:

● what

● when

● where

● who

● why.

Consider the benefits of asking more open questions in your everyday conversations. *What* difference do you think that will make? (And *how* could you start right now?)

Strategising or 'leading the witness'

Remember, in coaching we're encouraging others to be more self-directed. So our questions must also have an *open intention*. Questions with an open intention are unattached to any particular outcome or response. They include questions such as 'What do you think?' or 'What do you want?' Questions with a closed intention assume a more limited number of options as a response, for example 'What would your conscience tell you to do in order to not upset her further?' The question closes down the options of a response dramatically. Sometimes we do this to make the other person realise something we think is true, for example 'What are the integrity issues here?' When we ask a question where we know what we want someone to answer, it's a subtle form of direction or control.

> in coaching we're encouraging others to be more self-directed

Asking 'questions with a strategy' is an easy trap to fall into when we begin to learn to coach others. That's because we know we need to avoid being overly directive and let someone else come up with their own answers, but we still want to 'help' or guide someone to get to a solution. And so we ask 'strategising' questions instead. The following table includes examples of strategising questions, plus questions with a more open intention.

Strategised question	Question with a more open intention
Couldn't you speak to your boss about this?	What support do you need with this?
Have you considered putting a plan together to make everyone agree to the dates?	How can you get everyone to agree to the dates?
How angry are you about all this?	How are you feeling about this?
What could your HR representative do to help you?	Who else might help? [*Or even more open*] What are you thinking of doing?
Didn't you say that Dave doesn't actually want to be involved anyway?	How would Dave feel about that?

As you can see, the strategised questions appear to have more of an 'agenda' – as though the person asking them is 'getting at something' or has an opinion about what the answer should be. We sometimes call this 'leading the witness', because the person asking the question appears to be using a subtle form of direction to reach a predetermined conclusion. In coaching, these types of questions are much less effective than open questions, because they are directive in tone and reduce the creativity, engagement and commitment of the person being coached.

 **brilliant** tip

Why watch your voice?

A great question can be wrecked by lousy tonality. For example, try asking the question 'Why did you do that?' out loud in the following ways:

- with a frown, i.e. disapprovingly
- as if you think the person is the most stupid you've met in a long time
- in amazement, i.e. eyes wide
- with a big smile
- with a gentle, neutral tone.

This example also demonstrates the potential pitfall of using questions that begin with the word 'why', because they can cause people to be defensive or to feel they need to justify themselves. So remember to be careful using 'why' and be careful with your tonality. Try to stay neutral with your tone, so that the person feels less judged by the question and so will feel less cautious with their response.

Powerful questions

In coaching, powerful questions are an especially useful tool because they encompass a statement of problem and propel it towards a solution. In coaching, people sometimes get 'stuck' in a problem. A powerful question can turn someone's energy away from describing or justifying an issue and towards more constructive thought. Also, by adopting a solution focus we help lighten the mood of a situation – away from frustration and towards optimism.

A powerful question:

● acknowledges the issue or challenge
● assumes that a positive outcome is possible
● is open (what, how, etc.) and provokes a creative response.

In the workplace, we are often faced with complaints or issues that ignore the *possibility* of a solution, for example 'We can't do this' or 'This is an impossible situation'. As a coach (or a manager), much of the value you add is in the creation of a sense of possibility in a situation and the help you give to people to move towards a solution. The following table shows how you might use powerful questions in these types of situations.

Statement of issue/complaint	Powerful question
It's hopeless – we're never going to get it done by Friday because we've already got so much other work in the queue.	How can we get it done by Friday and still deal with the other work in the queue?
We'd love to have a staff summer party again, but the money needs to go on training this year.	How can we find the money for a summer party *and* still afford the training?
We really need to do some team building to improve collaboration, but people's roles are going to change and we don't yet know what that's going to mean.	How can we do some team building and still support the new roles in future?

 **brilliant** recap

Effective questioning

In coaching, effective questioning provokes valuable thoughts and reflection, helps insight to surface or helps someone decide and act. Effective questions are simply worded so that the person answering needs only to work on forming their response, rather than on their understanding of the question. Effective questions also have a clear sense of purpose, for example to gather more information, see something from another perspective, or create a sense of the future. It's important that questions have a predominantly open intention, i.e. they are unattached to any predetermined outcome. When our questions are open, simple and have a clear purpose, coachees can respond creatively and effectively.

CHAPTER 7

A flexible style of influence

Build rapport or relationship

Constructive feedback

Focused listening

Flexible style of influence

Effective questioning

n our fourth skill, we'll reflect on the need to develop a flexible style of influence. We'll look at the different ways you influence someone during a conversation and consider a range of methods in which to do that. We'll build on previous principles, e.g. directive and less directive styles, and show how it's not always necessary to choose between the two: sometimes you can move between or combine styles. As you'd expect, there will be hints, tips and guidance to encourage you to get the most from the ideas on offer.

What do we mean by 'flexible style of influence'?

As a quick reminder, there are two basic 'ends' to our spectrum of influence as Figure 7.1 illustrates.

Directive

Self-directed

- I know how
- I tell you
- You follow instruction

- You know how
- I ask you
- You decide

Figure 7.1 Spectrum of influence

Why is flexibility important to develop?

You will remember that coaching is a conversation that influences the thoughts, behaviour and learning of another person. We have already seen that your ability to adopt a less directive style of conversation with people will help them engage with ideas, feel listened to and learn things for themselves. On the other hand, a coaching conversation isn't just one person asking lots of questions of another. Just consider that idea for a moment: all you're allowed to do during a conversation is ask questions, nothing else; just a list of questions. In the role of questioner, the conversation might feel constraining and even frustrating. You'll want to say things, make observations perhaps, but feel like you're not 'allowed' to do that. As a manager, you might be hearing things that don't make sense, or that you know you can't allow to happen. For the person being coached, a list of questions with no 'input' from the manager might feel odd, unnatural and potentially put them under pressure. The conversation needs to feel natural for you and natural for the person you're with.

> coaching shouldn't mean you have an apparent 'personality change'

Coaching someone shouldn't mean you have an apparent 'personality change', or lose your natural, easy-going style. So, to stay effective as a coach and retain your sense of comfort during conversations, you need to use other behaviours. This will help you move from being more directive when that feels right, to relaxing towards being less directive and encouraging the coachee to think for themselves when that is more appropriate.

Two ends of a scale, with behaviours in between . . .

Some language is clearly directive and attempts to exert a directive style of influence, e.g. 'I want you to do this'. Other language allows an individual to decide for themselves, e.g. 'What do you want to do?' Between these two extremes are behaviours that exert different 'strengths' of influence. For example, if I make an observation on or about something you

have said, this will have a more 'neutral' impact on you than if I
gave you direct advice (see Figure 7.2).

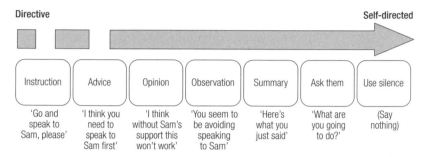

Figure 7.2 Scale of influence

Let's take a look at the different behaviours on the above scale
and reflect on how you might use them productively. We'll start
with the less directive behaviours and move towards the more
directive end of the scale (from right to left of the figure).

 **questions**

How much flexibility do you have?

Use the following questions to increase your self-awareness in this area.
Another way to do this would be to have someone observe how you
typically influence others, e.g. in a meeting, and then ask them to answer
the questions on your behalf.

ⓠ During a typical conversation, what seems more important: giving
   your opinion or making an effort to understand someone else's?

ⓠ How often do you simply summarise what someone's said, without
   adding your own opinion or ideas immediately afterwards?

ⓠ How often do you make observations about what someone is saying,
   simply to draw their attention to something that might help them,
   i.e. without following up with your own view?

Finally, spend a little time reflecting on how much you feel compelled to
influence at all. For example, are you comfortable simply to facilitate a
conversation with no input on the content of that conversation?

Behaviour 1: Say nothing

The behaviour of 'saying nothing' is a little strange to imagine as an influencing style, yet silence as a response to what someone has just said can sometimes be perfect. Silence enables someone to pause, reflect on what they've just said, or perhaps go deeper into what they are saying. It suggests calmness from you and allows the other person to relax and speak from the sense of ease that you have created. It also helps you to really listen to the other person, perhaps observing their body language or energy. Like most of the behaviours described here, overusing this technique can have the reverse effect and cause the other person to feel tense because you're not responding to them verbally. You'll know when a silence becomes uncomfortable for the person you're coaching by their non-verbal signals, e.g. changes in their posture, tone or facial expressions. Some signals you receive will be clear indications that you need to speak, e.g. if they stop speaking, or look directly back at you with an expectant expression, whereas others are more subtle.

Behaviour 2: Ask an open – neutrally worded – question

For a question to have the least directive style of influence, it should be both open and worded as neutrally as possible. For example, 'Do you think you should plan the meeting in advance with Bill?' is not open as it can be answered simply with a yes or no. The question also attempts to be directive: you're suggesting they should plan the meeting. A more neutral question might be: 'How do you think you need to prepare for the meeting?' Although this question is still slightly directive, as you're suggesting preparation is necessary, it may be both appropriate and helpful (to help someone think the preparation through) or you may be guiding the person too specifically or strongly, for example because they need to talk about some other aspect of the meeting first. As with all of these principles, you are the best judge of your situations and will be able to decide when you need to have a more direct influence on the conversation. A third, very neutral question in that situation would be: 'What thoughts are you having now?' This may be too vague but, on the other hand, could be just perfect to help them think. Again, your internal sense of what's best to do is one that you need to develop.

> your internal sense of what's best to do is one that you need to develop

 **brilliant** tip

Your body will help you if you let it!

After 15 years of coaching others and discussing this with other coaches, I've learnt that the following is 'strange but true'.

Your body can often help as an indicator of how a conversation is going, or even act as a guide to suggest what you should do next. Learn to 'tune in' to your body during coaching conversations, particularly your head, shoulders and torso, so that you can check occasionally to see how it corresponds to what's happening. For example:

● If the conversation is 'in flow', i.e. going well, how does your body feel?

● When you know something's not 'right', how does your body feel?

● When you need to make a decision, e.g. to stay quiet or to speak, how does your body help you to do that?

As you gain an increasing awareness of – or connection to – your body, you'll learn to trust and be guided by it. For example, maybe I've been talking about someone's team for a long time and get a growing sense that the conversation feels 'hollow', or as if the conversation isn't going anywhere. When I check my body, I have a feeling that resonates, or is noticeable in some way. Perhaps there's lightness in my stomach or shoulders, or maybe the top of my head feels odd. Or maybe I'll consider asking a certain question but my stomach feels heavy when I think about it, so I'll stay quiet.

▶

These are just a few of my signals – how your body communicates with you will be distinct to you. The signals from your body are a way to access your natural intuition and can be a real enhancement to your coaching ability. Your awareness may take a little time to grow until you can fully trust your senses, but it will make a positive difference to your efficiency and results as a coach.

Behaviour 3: Summarise what you've been hearing

Summarising what the person you're coaching has said can be helpful for you as a listener and also for the person you are listening to. For you, it enables you to demonstrate that you've understood the key points of what someone has said, and so confirms mutual understanding. It also helps you to draw the other person's attention to what you are suggesting are the key facts of the situation, and to 'filter out' any less relevant facts simply by not mentioning them. For the other person, you're giving them a rest from talking and space to reflect on what they've been saying. By 'standing back' and listening to their own situation from your perspective, the other person is able to gain a more objective view of key facts or events. It might surprise you how much benefit people get from this simple tool; when they hear what they've just been saying, they have additional insights or reach conclusions they might not have found otherwise.

 **brilliant** tip

Less is more

Giving summaries can be so obviously beneficial in a situation that it becomes an overused tool. Too many summaries during a conversation can slow progress and potentially frustrate the person who is trying to describe their situations or views. Use the following principles to help guide you as to when a summary might be appropriate.

- When you haven't spoken for a long time and you're experiencing a sense of becoming disconnected with the person talking, e.g. they've lost eye contact with you and seem to be talking almost to themselves.
- When you feel that the conversation is rambling or going round in circles, i.e. the same or similar facts seem to be being repeated.
- When you're a little confused by what you're hearing and want to check you understand what the other person is saying or feeling.
- When you think that the other person is becoming fatigued or confused and might appreciate a rest from talking, or benefit from some time to reflect.
- When you particularly want to draw the other person's attention to something they've said, e.g. a word or phrase or sentiment.

Behaviour 4: Make an observation

An observation is when you notice something that the other person has said and choose to draw their attention to it. It has a stronger influence than a summary, because you have a clear reason for drawing their attention to it. Perhaps they have contradicted themselves in an interesting way, or maybe they've been using a certain phrase or negative language repeatedly and not heard themselves doing that. Some of your observations might be neutral, or purely factual. Some of your observations will have more of your interpretation or opinion blended into them, as the table below illustrates.

Observation	Objective or subjective?
You've mentioned three times that the meeting on Monday might be difficult, or tough in some way.	This is factual and allows the other person to judge the importance or relevance.
You seem to be dreading the meeting on Monday.	This is your observation that interprets their feelings behind what they've been saying.
The meeting on Monday seems to be more important to this conversation than the original topic you wanted to discuss.	This is more interpretation by you and clearly more directive of what you think should happen next.

Once again, any of the above may be valid choices, depending on the situation and what seems helpful for the other person.

Behaviour 5: Give an opinion

Giving an opinion is offering your view of someone else's situation or conversation, drawing upon your thoughts, knowledge and experience. This is more directive than giving a summary or making an observation, as you are 'judging' the situation and attempting to influence someone's own view or decisions. Some opinions are more forceful than others, and the type of opinion you offer relies on:

● your sound judgement of a situation

● the warmth of rapport you have with the person you are coaching

● the appetite or potential of the other person to hear your opinion and be open to it.

The table below illustrates this.

Your opinion	Strength of 'directiveness' or risk of rejection
I wonder if Geoff might be a little uncomfortable with his role on the project.	This is subtly worded to be almost a question to ponder rather than an opinion. Depending on the individual and the situation, this may be useful, or easily ignored!
I think Geoff sounds like he's uncomfortable with his role on the project.	This is simple, clear and to the point; it's 'owned' as an opinion, i.e. 'I think'.
Geoff's clearly very uncomfortable with his role on the project.	This is more assertive, pointed and so 'directive' or suggesting of action.

brilliant tip

Develop flexibility by relaxing your own habits

This chapter describes a range of behaviours in order to paint a fuller picture of that range. You will, however, already use some of these behaviours, perhaps out of habit and without noticing. Perhaps you give opinions, advice and instruction naturally but rarely summarise or offer simple observations in order to help someone else think. To develop your true flexibility, try the following.

● First, increase your self-awareness by noticing how you typically influence during conversations, or maybe ask a colleague to observe you, e.g. in meetings.

● Next, decide on a period of time during which you will avoid using your typical behaviours, such as giving opinion or advice, to force yourself to use other responses, such as summarising or making observations. Again, it may be helpful to share with a trusted colleague what you intend to do.

● Finally, notice the difference this makes, perhaps asking a colleague for feedback, e.g. 'Did this work? What difference does it make?'

When you've given this a try, simply decide for yourself which behaviours might add the most to how you influence people. Remember, the aim of doing this is to influence people in a way that helps people think and act for themselves. So when you're reviewing 'Does this work?' you need to notice if you did that – or not!

Behaviour 6: Give advice

When you give advice, you tell the other person what you think they should do, accepting that they might not actually do it. This is much the same as you might do with a friend, e.g. 'If I were you …' or 'What I would do is …' Advice is different from opinion because there is a clearer intention to affect the behaviour of another person. To be an effective coach, you should give advice only sparingly and with caution. As you already know, coaching leans away from telling people what they 'should or could do' in favour of helping them to think through a situation and decide for themselves. Particularly in the early days of learning to coach, I would encourage you to try not to give advice; instead develop your ability to be non-directive. However, it's also true that there may be times when your advice is relevant, useful and supportive and so is exactly what's needed in the situation. The table below will help you reflect on the different 'strengths' of advice, from allowing the coachee to retain self-direction to giving almost a directive instruction.

Your advice	Level of 'directiveness'
I wonder if you might benefit from a conversation with the HR department.	This is subtly worded and almost 'offers' the advice as something that can easily be rejected.
I think you should go and speak to the HR department.	This is simple, clear and to the point; it is also owned, i.e. 'I think'.
It's really important that you speak to the HR department and get some expert input here.	This is assertive and pointed, and so is 'directive' or suggesting of action.

Please remember that if you are a person's manager or boss any advice from you may feel like an instruction to them. Your subordinates might expect, or feel that they need, instructions or solutions from you. If you can see this is the case with some people you work with, you may choose to put 'advice' in the same category as instructions, because they create the same directive effect on those people. Another option might be to signal that the advice isn't instruction, e.g. 'This is just gentle advice – you must decide what's best for you here.'

Behaviour 7: Give an instruction

As you'd expect, when you instruct someone to do something, you attempt to influence their actions by directive means. Interestingly, some instructions are stronger than others. Some instructions prescribe specific, detailed actions, while other 'instructions' tell people how best to work things out for themselves. So you can use a directive instruction to help someone to be self-directed! The table below explains this apparent contradiction.

The instruction	Directive or encourages self-direction?
Go and speak to Jon and ask him to reschedule the meeting.	Clearly a directive instruction (or request), it suggests that you know what should happen and that you are telling someone to do that.
OK, take the rest of the day to figure out a solution to this. Get back to me by the end of the day and let me know what you're proposing to do.	This is clearly directive and yet expects the other person to provide a solution. It may put the person under some pressure, which may or may not work well.
Go and speak to Jon and figure out a solution that you both agree on, and then let me know what you want to do.	Although this is a directive instruction, it still allows the other person a level of empowerment – to decide for themselves what they are going to do.

Please remember that the above statements can all have different effects dependent on your manner and tone of voice when you make them. For example, a harsh, punchy, snappy tone has a far different impact from a warmer, relaxed one. Try saying the above statements out loud using different styles of speech to explore your own impact further.

 recap

A flexible style of influence

It's both unnatural and impractical for your coaching conversations to be merely a list of questions from you, where you allow other people to decide what to do and how to do it. As a manager, you need to be able to balance empowering people with a need to stay practical, within the rules, etc. This means that you need to develop the flexibility to use different methods of influence, both with different people and during the conversations themselves. Being able to use intermediate behaviours, such as giving summaries, making observations and offering opinions, that are neither totally directive nor totally non-directive, will help you do this.

CHAPTER 8

Constructive feedback

Build rapport or relationship

Constructive feedback

Focused listening

Flexible style of influence

Effective questioning

I n our fifth and final skill we'll cover the topic of giving constructive feedback. We'll use some fresh principles and perspectives to offer new ideas about what may be a familiar topic. In this chapter we'll cover what we mean by feedback, the principles of giving constructive feedback, plus some of the natural barriers we might encounter. As usual I'll offer hints, tips and guidance, as well as some exercises to encourage your learning in this area.

If you are more interested in the logical stages or sequence of a feedback conversation, then go straight to Chapter 10 on page 143. There you'll find the process plus a worked example that includes dialogue.

What do we mean by feedback?

To give feedback to someone is to give them information. In common use, feedback is normally information or opinion given to a person who is related to that information or opinion. For example, I've just given a presentation and you tell me your view of my performance – what worked, didn't work, etc. Or I've been working for you for six months and you want to have a general conversation about how things are going, and offer opinion from your perspective.

Feedback has a poor reputation

In the workplace, the term 'feedback' is sometimes used to disguise a piece of criticism. In its worst form it may even be an act of aggression, if we use the 'polite' term of 'feedback' to 'have a go' at someone. The phrase 'I'd like to give you some feedback, please' can provoke feelings of doubt or dread in the person about to receive that feedback. That's because they probably imagine they are about to be criticised in some way, or think they are 'in trouble'. It's a shame, because feedback can be exactly the opposite of that – as I hope to demonstrate.

 questions

What do you feel about feedback?

Use the following questions to identify the beliefs you have about feedback. Allow your mind to wander and imagine the scenarios fully.

Q Imagine a colleague approaches you and says, 'Have you got a few minutes ... I'd like to give you some feedback.' How would you feel?

Q Identify someone you work with who might benefit from receiving feedback about something. Now imagine that you've decided to give them that feedback. What do you imagine happening?

Q In either of the above examples, did you imagine that any of the feedback messages might be positive?

Finally, spend a little time reflecting on how your beliefs about feedback may affect your ability both to give it and to receive it.

Is it worse to give than to receive?

Many of us dislike giving feedback even more than receiving it. We tend to focus on the potential negative response of the person to whom we're giving feedback, and that causes us discomfort. We may anticipate that the person receiving the feedback will think badly of us or reject us for having given them feedback. We might also be concerned that they will get emotional, perhaps defensive, hostile or upset.

Don't think about the blue rabbit

Ironically, our mental preparation for things going badly actually increases the chances of their going badly. That's because our mind draws us towards what we think most about. For example, if I tell you *not* to think about the blue rabbit wearing sunglasses (no, *don't* think about the blue rabbit, the one wearing sunglasses), isn't that just what you think about?

Before giving feedback we often use our creative genius to invent nightmarish scenarios and then try to have them 'not' happen. But then, just like telling ourselves *not* to think about the blue rabbit, that's what we focus on. For example, you're preparing to have a conversation with a chatterbox in your team, called Sophie. She's really quite loud, with a laugh you find irritating. As you're preparing to have the conversation you're thinking: 'When I'm telling her about her behaviour, don't say "shrieking", "irritating" or "cackle" – that would sound too personal. Definitely not "shrieking" or "cackle" – that would be terrible.' Then, when you have the conversation with Sophie and she asks you to describe what you mean, aren't they the *only* words you can think of?

Solution: focus on what you want

There's a simple solution to this issue: focus on what you want, instead of what you don't want. For example, in your conversation with Sophie, if you want to use words like 'bubbly, talkative and enthusiastic', think about those words. Put your attention on to how you want things to be; it's a simple switch that can alter your course in a conversation dramatically. It also works for feelings too. Perhaps you decide you want to feel calm as you give feedback, so think, 'OK, I'm going to feel calm and relaxed now.' Then build that idea further: think about what it's like to feel calm and relaxed and how that's going to be in the situation. For example: 'Right, I can imagine myself feeling calm and relaxed as I'm talking to her. I can imagine things going well.' As you focus on how things will be when they go well, then you will automatically draw yourself closer to that outcome.

focus on what you want, instead of what you don't want

What's fabulous about feedback?

By turning our attention to what's great about good feedback and how much value it can be to people, not only do we immediately feel better about it but we also increase our chances of giving great feedback that others value. Here are just a few of the positive benefits of giving your colleagues at work constructive feedback.

● People appreciate your commitment to and support of their development (especially where they think you've made a real effort to give it).

● We often enjoy talking about ourselves, especially when it helps us to get better at something. Imagine your manager never bothered to tell you how you were doing – how would that feel?

● We relish learning. We want to feel as though we're making progress in an area, especially where it's a personal challenge that we feel is worthwhile.

What are the key principles of feedback?

Most of the principles that follow relate to messages that can be either 'positive' or 'negative'. Both of those terms are subjective. For example: you receive the feedback that you seem to place more importance on progressing tasks than on how people are feeling; I might call that negative but you might find it positive. So let's assume that by positive we mean complimentary statements, and by negative we mean more difficult messages of a 'problem' or a need for improvement. In either case, the following principles apply, especially when giving messages that are more difficult to hear.

Preparation: why, what, how

Before you give feedback, make sure that you're well prepared and focused on a positive outcome. For example, what are the precise messages you want to give? How and where do you plan to deliver the messages? Also, think a little about how the other person is likely to respond, i.e. how they might feel. Consider the best way to approach the person, given your knowledge of them and the situation. You may choose not to use the word 'feedback' at all, perhaps saying instead 'Can we have a chat about the meeting yesterday? I'd like to talk about how that went.'

For a fuller list of preparation points, see the checklist at the end of this chapter.

Feeling buoyant, staying 'above zero'

Your emotional state will help or hinder your ability to think, speak and react resourcefully during the conversation. Let's imagine that there's a range of emotional states that you might place at different points on a numbered scale. Anything above zero is generally positive – for example calm, relaxed, confident – and zero is neutral. 'Below zero' might be more negative feelings of hesitation, trepidation, or even annoyance and frustration. I would encourage you to give feedback when you are feeling emotionally stable and with a sense of balance or optimism about the situation (especially if you're delivering a tough message). Your emotional balance also influences the person you are talking to, and will support them to receive the messages you are offering.

> your emotional state will help or hinder your ability to think, speak and react

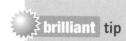 **tip**

Creating confidence

If you are finding it difficult to reach 'above zero', for example to feel calm and focused, try some or all of the following.

● Go for a walk to think things through – maybe there's a thought or idea you need to have that will ease its way out as you relax.

● Decide how you want to feel and create that feeling – use your breathing and posture if that helps. For example, if you want to feel confident, then walk confidently, breathe confidently and adopt the physical posture of how you typically are when you're feeling relaxed and confident.

● Focus on a positive outcome – imagine the conversation going well, and see yourself as you want to be. See, hear and feel what that will be like.

● Get a trusted colleague to help you prepare – either talk things through or, better still, rehearse. Rehearsal is the best way I know of ironing out any creases in a planned conversation.

● Consider not giving the feedback – just allow yourself to imagine that you don't give the feedback after all. Does that feel better or not? Is your relief temporary or lasting? If you decide not to give the feedback, remember to check whether you've decided to do the right thing or just the easy thing. That way you'll know if your decision is good enough for you.

Given with positive intention

Consider your own intentions. Are they positive? Consider giving the feedback, then ask yourself 'How might the other person benefit?' That benefit might be personal growth, progress on a task, or their performance at work generally. Once you're clear about what the benefit might be for the individual, you have the option of sharing that with them if it's appropriate; for example, 'I'm hoping this might take some of the pressure off you to have all the answers sometimes.' If your motivation for giving feedback seems to be based on your emotional state, for example, 'I'm really annoyed with them' or 'I just can't bear them as a person', then you need to reflect further and find an objective viewpoint to guide you. If you are unable to find this objective view now, you are less likely to remain impartial during the conversation.

Own your own message, speak your own truth

If your reason for feedback is that someone else thinks it's a good idea, I'd suggest caution. For example, Gill works for you and is complaining about Bruce, who also works for you. Gill complains that on the days that you're not in the office Bruce shows up late and she'd like you to 'tackle' him about it. While you have no reason to doubt Gill is telling the truth (you trust her), this is not a huge issue with you personally. Bruce is one of the stronger performing members of the team. The only real issue is that Gill feels the situation is unfair and expects you, as manager, to ensure that 'fairness reigns'. Your issue is more a question of integrity. For example, do you try to calm Gill down about this, in the hope that the issue goes away? Or do you have a conversation with Bruce and risk creating a real issue? After all, Bruce may feel aggrieved that someone has complained about him and be suspicious of all the team if the individual isn't open about it. Or Bruce may reject accusations against him as untrue, in which case it will be very difficult to make progress – unless Gill speaks up.

Feedback should be attributed to and owned by the person with the issue. One valid option is to encourage Gill to offer feedback herself. Explain your reasons and also the risks of your giving feedback to Bruce in this type of circumstance. In exceptional circumstances, i.e. where

> feedback should be attributed to and owned by the person with the issue

you simply cannot avoid giving a message, then you have the option of acting as a mediator in the situation. For example, 'I'm having this conversation on behalf of James because he doesn't feel able to raise it with you personally.' James needs to know that you're doing this, and both James and the person you're giving feedback to need to be encouraged to stay constructive afterwards. This might mean you facilitating a conversation between them, or encouraging that they talk things through in a constructive way.

Objective not subjective

Being objective means we strip out as much personal judgement as possible, leaving only the bare facts of the situation. Subjective statements rely more on the accuracy of personal judgement and can more easily be rejected or refuted. Objective statements tend to be more neutral, as they are more accurate and so more easily accepted.

Let's assume that you've decided to give a colleague called Mark some feedback about his tendency to make commitments and then not keep them. It's important to give this message in an objective, not subjective, way. The statements in the following table illustrate this.

Subjective statement	Objective statement
I'm not sure if you're coping or not – I just get the feeling that you're not.	Our last few conversations have mainly been about things that are being delivered late.
You don't deliver things when you say you're going to – it makes a mockery of our planning process, and yesterday was a disaster.	I've had some experiences recently where I've had to chase you for things you said you'd deliver – the missing data yesterday has caused us to push out the dates on our plan.

As you can see, the objective statements seem more 'factual'. Perhaps the terms 'last few' or 'some experiences' are a little vague and the actual number might work better, for example 'three'. I've not used the actual amount in an effort to give a 'lighter' message. We want to progress the conversation towards solution, rather than 'make someone wrong'. For a better idea of the structure and stages of a conversation, see Chapter 10 on page 143.

Comment on behaviour not personality

Constructive feedback comments on behaviour rather than the person or their personality. For example, 'You're overbearing' attacks the person, whereas 'Sometimes you talk over people' comments on their behaviour. Generally we feel we have choice about what we do, but have much less choice about who we are. So give messages based on observations of behaviour, rather than judgements of the person or their personality. The table below gives further examples.

Comments on person	Comments on behaviour
You're rubbish at keeping commitments.	Sometimes you don't keep your commitments.
I find you controlling.	I'd like you to listen to my ideas more often.
You're stubborn.	I'd like you to respond more flexibly sometimes.

Balanced message

Aim to give balanced messages where appropriate, i.e. 'positives' with 'negatives'. But only do that if the positives relate to the negatives in some way, and you can deliver the positives in a *genuine, natural way*. By natural I mean in a way that feels natural for the conversation, in flow with what's being discussed. The following example comes part-way through a conversation with Tanya, after her manager has told her that, in meetings, Tanya voices her own ideas with great passion and conviction and often ignores or interrupts the input of others.

> *Manager*   Tanya, I'll add that I do value your energy in these meetings – you're able to get everyone behind a situation, which is great – it's just that sometimes some of the quieter members of the team seem less able to offer ideas, and if possible I'd like to gain their input on these things.

The manager has balanced the negative point with a positive acknowledgement (that they value Tanya's energy) while not detracting from the main message. We aim to acknowledge positive attributes and behaviours where it's appropriate. By doing so, we create a sense of perspective on a situation and help the person receiving feedback remain buoyant. What works much less well is when we try to think of something positive and put it into the conversation in a phoney attempt to 'prop up' a bleak message. So keep positive messages genuine!

> **acknowledge positive attributes and behaviours where it's appropriate**

brilliant tip

Slight of mouth

It's often more helpful to tell someone what you'd prefer rather than what you don't like. For example, 'Don't talk so much' becomes 'Listen to other people's ideas more often'. It helps someone to focus on the solution, rather than get 'stuck' in the problem. It's a subtle switch, but one that can work really well.

Check for understanding and engagement

Checking for understanding and engagement helps the other person to confirm that they have understood what you have said and also involves them in the conversation. It may be as simple as asking 'How does this sound?' or 'What are your thoughts about this?' or 'Have you thought about this before?' Questions are best kept deliberately vague, to enable someone to enter into the conversation, without feeling a pressure to answer in any particular way.

This is a good way of maintaining rapport and making the feedback effective. When we check for understanding and engagement, we also take the pressure off ourselves to keep talking, and we allow the other person to offer their views or responses. It turns the conversation into a conversation, rather than one person talking *at* another. The key is to remember to do it at an appropriate point in the conversation, i.e. after the message of feedback has been given. The following example comes part-way through the conversation with Tanya again, just after the manager has described her tendency to talk over people in meetings.

Manager So basically it's about the impact this has on others, and also possibly the overall balance of conversation in the meeting. Can I ask what your thoughts about this are?

Tanya Well, I guess I'm a bit taken aback by this, I mean I didn't realise it's an issue. I certainly didn't think that other people might stay quiet just because of what I'm saying.

Manager Right [neutral tone followed by silence].

Tanya I mean, you just expect that if people have something to say then they say it – I know that's what I do. Why can't they do that?

Here the manager is giving Tanya a chance to express herself and also process some of her reactions to the feedback. Her initial reactions may not be her final response, and so the manager doesn't react to them. Instead the manager uses silence to allow Tanya to voice her immediate thoughts. But if the manager had simply kept talking, explaining the situation and leaving Tanya no room to respond, then Tanya may feel suppressed in the conversation. Remember, a coaching manager operates from a position of equality with the people they manage. So it's important that this is a conversation between two adults, rather than a lecture from one to the other.

> a coaching manager operates from a position of equality with the people they manage

Help them decide on a way forward

Using the previous point of an 'adult-to-adult' conversation, it's best if actions or next steps are agreed in collaboration rather than as an instruction from the manager. Helping someone else to decide will allow them to engage with what they feel is a good way forward that works for them. You're obviously able to offer views on their decisions if you want, but be cautious. Sometimes it's better to let someone proceed with what you think is a flawed plan rather than dismiss the plan in favour of your own. After all, most issues can be given time and so you don't need to find what *you* think is a perfect solution. Your own wisdom will help you to decide when to challenge and when to let go.

The following example continues the previous scenario and offers an appropriate balance from the manager in terms of challenge and 'letting go'.

Manager   So, having thought a little about this now, what are your options, do you think?

Tanya   Well, I'm tempted just to stay quiet, and then no one can say I'm not letting anyone else speak!

Manager   Well, it's an option, but given that I really value your input, it's probably not great longer term. What else could you do?

Tanya   Well, I don't know – be more aware of others I suppose. I mean, I'm certainly going to think about it. I just need to realise when others have something to say.

Manager OK, how do you see that working?

Tanya   I guess I need to learn to stop talking a bit more quickly, or get to the point quicker. I'm not sure – I'm going to have to think about this.

Manager I think it sounds like you're on the right track, and yes you'd want to think about it wouldn't you? I'm not sure it takes any more than that.

The manager is again using a very light touch in the conversation. They don't need to prescribe a list of agreed actions, for example talk to other people, write a list, etc. The manager knows that this is an issue of self-awareness first, which will need some reflection time. They also trust that Tanya is engaged with the topic and wants to do something about it. The manager is assuming that Tanya is a mature adult and will work on this issue afterwards. They also know that if the behaviour remains the same, then they have the opportunity to revisit the topic and can do so on a firmer footing.

After this, all the manager needs to do is close the conversation in a way that demonstrates ongoing support and commitment.

Manager Tanya, I'm wondering what support you might need from me for this?

Tanya   [pauses] Nothing right now – maybe there might be something later, but right now it's fine.

Manager OK, good. Well, let me know. So are we all right to leave this here?

So the manager has offered some initial feedback, left it with Tanya to reflect and then act on, while leaving the topic open for future debate. If the manager sees a continuation of the issue, they can simply revisit the conversation. Conversely, if the manager sees improvements, then they'll want to acknowledge those in a genuine way. By these acknowledgements of progress, Tanya can view what might have been an uncomfortable conversation as actually one that was really valuable to her.

 **checklist**

Plan to succeed!

Before you next give someone feedback, take a few moments to consider the following.

● Why do you want to give feedback – how might it benefit the other person?

● Is this your own feedback or someone else's? Can you 'own' the messages as your own?

● What are the key messages you want to give – are they objective and based on behaviour?

● How, where and when do you plan to give the messages – are the timing and situation appropriate?

● How are you feeling about giving the feedback, i.e. are you 'above zero' emotionally?

● What are the outcomes from the conversation that you hope to achieve?

● How might the person receiving the observations react to this feedback?

Once you've given feedback, you might like to reflect on how well it went, or what you might want to do differently next time. If you're really brave, you might even ask the person to whom you gave the feedback for some feedback!

 **brilliant** recap

Constructive feedback

Most of us would choose to receive constructive feedback – which supports our ability to learn, develop and be successful – on a regular basis. So giving constructive, motivating feedback becomes a necessary tool for any effective manager. The challenge for managers is to offer these messages using a balanced, natural style so that people can welcome and engage with them. And where we want to develop a coaching style of manager, i.e. one who makes the development of others important, then giving regular, constructive feedback is essential.

PART 3

Application

I n this part of the book we'll look at the different ways you might use coaching in your workplace. We'll look at planned coaching conversations as well as coaching as a natural response to everyday conversations and questions. You'll find structures of conversation as well as sample dialogue, to help you link principles to actual behaviour.

This part is intended to be read selectively, according to your needs, rather than read from front to back. I've given you four different scenarios in which coaching might happen, to show how coaching fits within each one. All the basic coaching principles discussed so far stay the same; it's just your objectives for having the conversation that might be slightly different. I'd advise that you first become familiar with what type of circumstance each scenario caters for, before deciding how much you want to read. That way you can start with what's most relevant to you, and pick up on the other scenarios as you need them. A little like a recipe book perhaps – you can flick though and see what you fancy, and what most suits you right now. And of course you can revisit any scenario in the future, as a guide for a particular situation when it crops up.

You'll find a summary of what each scenario does below. First let me explain how coaching occurs in the workplace.

Where and when can coaching happen?

Coaching can happen in both on-line and off-line situations. It's useful to highlight the differences between those situations, as the structures that support them can be slightly different. By structures I simply mean the logical sets of activities that create a map for your conversational journey. The idea of a 'beginning, middle and end' to what might be a conversation lasting an hour or more will help to guide you through the different stages. For example, if you have regular one-to-one update meetings with subordinates, I have a simple structure called the Coaching Path to help you navigate that conversation. If, however, you sit in a busy work environment and want to coach more 'on-line', then your approach will be different. So I'll offer you a shorter structure for those 'bite-sized' conversations, i.e. where your coaching conversations may last 60 seconds or less. I call this shorter structure Response Coaching.

On-line or off-line – a useful distinction

The terms 'on-line' and 'off-line' are used to describe activities either in the heart of the action or away from it. For example, if we are at our desks engaged in the daily task of checking invoices, that's an on-line activity. If we walk away from that operational situation and sit in a meeting room with colleagues to discuss those invoices, that's an off-line activity. Both terms are imperfect as some activities appear one way but may actually be another, for example taking a pile of invoices into a meeting room to work quietly – it's sort of an off-line on-line activity! But let's assume that generally when we talk about on-line, we mean activities in a live working environment that are being carried out as part of everyday business. And by off-line we refer to discussions or meetings that happen away from the operational work environment, perhaps in meeting rooms, canteens or anywhere away from our normal work base.

Where do you want to start coaching?

Now all you need to decide is, what are the situations in which you want to begin using coaching principles and behaviours? Use the following descriptions to help you choose which scenario most closely matches the type of coaching you might want to do first.

Chapter 9: Off-line session when the coachee has the topic or agenda

This scenario is a scheduled meeting with a subordinate, where you want them to 'own' the session and be responsible for setting the objectives and desired outcome. Ideally they will come prepared with an idea of what they want to get from their time with you. And if they don't, you'll simply help them work out what they want to get from the meeting in the first few minutes. This scenario enables more 'pure coaching' from the manager, as the subordinate is encouraged to be responsible right from the start. We will be using the Coaching Path to guide you through this conversation.

Chapter 10: Off-line session when the manager has the topic or agenda

This scenario also uses the Coaching Path. This is a meeting or conversation with a subordinate where you, as the manager, 'own' the agenda, i.e. you know what you want to get from the meeting and want to adopt a coaching style during the conversation. Here, we're primarily referring to conversations relating to someone's performance, where you may want to give constructive feedback (which will include some tougher messages or areas for development). The key difference is that the manager initiates the conversation and knows what they want to get from it, for example raise an issue or encourage change. The challenge is to facilitate the conversation in a coaching style, for example by being less directive. So you'll want to engage the subordinate in the conversation as soon as possible in order to create a collaborative session rather than a reprimand. If you're looking for how to give feedback in a coaching style – this is the one.

Chapter 11: Off-line session when both the coachee and the manager have things to discuss

This is a meeting with a colleague or subordinate where the subordinate has objectives for the conversation and so do you. As manager, your agenda is less to give tough messages or developmental feedback and more around simple agenda items, for example 'I'd like an update on how "x" is going'. By blending the principles of the previous two scenarios, we are able to flex between the two. This scenario also uses the structure of the Coaching Path.

Chapter 12: On-line conversation – Response Coaching in a live environment

This scenario shows how coaching can occur as a natural behavioural response by a manager in a busy work environment. When faced with quick questions, issues or even complaints, managers can choose to coach issues rather than fix them. Using the Response Coaching model, coaching can become as easy as one, two, three. If you're managing a busy team and frequently get asked questions, or are expected to solve problems, this scenario is for you!

CHAPTER 9

Off-line: when the coachee has the topic or agenda

L et's imagine that one of your team wants to talk to you about something and they want to do it away from the workplace. Perhaps they're struggling with an issue or are frustrated about a situation and want to discuss this with you. It may be something apparently trivial, like a minor concern about a deadline, or something more significant, such as a crisis of confidence. It may be a fairly brief conversation, for example 20 minutes, or something that lasts much longer, perhaps several hours.

The Coaching Path

For all three off-line scenarios, we're going to use one basic structure. This structure is illustrated in Figure 9.1.

While the Coaching Path has five stages, the first and last stage will already be familiar to you. These stages are simply about beginning and ending a conversation. We'll explain these in brief to make sure you feel comfortable about opening and closing the session. The key stages that distinguish this conversation as a coaching conversation are the middle three stages, which we'll cover a little more thoroughly.

Let's now use the Coaching Path to help you navigate an off-line coaching conversation.

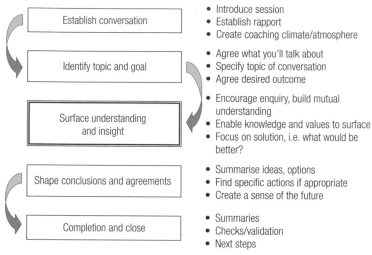

Figure 9.1 The Coaching Path

 **checklist**

Off-line: key coaching principles

Here's a quick reminder of the key principles that support an off-line coaching conversation.

● This is an 'adult-to-adult' conversation, i.e. you are both mature and equal in the conversation.

● The other person is responsible both for the issue they are surfacing and for their actions in relation to that issue – not in a 'blame' sense, but simply because they are empowered to think and act.

● The subordinate owns the agenda, i.e. they know what they want to discuss and also what they want to get out of the meeting.

● The subordinate probably has their own solution to the situation, or can be challenged to create a way forward for themselves.

● You add value to the conversation by facilitating their thoughts and ideas, using effective questioning to provoke thought and also offering your observations and feedback.

- Although you might have advice you could offer, you prefer that they come up with solutions. You're prepared not to give answers until it becomes silly not to. Even then, you'll make 'gentle offers', for example 'Can I offer a thought?'

Stage 1: Establish conversation

This step is about creating an appropriate sense of the conversation, e.g. 'We're here to discuss a work-related topic'.

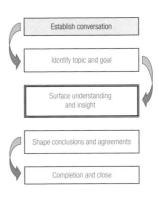

Remember it's a conversation of equals, rather than a meeting with the head of school, so think about how to adopt an 'adult-to-adult' posture and tone. Remember the importance of rapport and warmth. You want to create a relaxed yet professional tone to the conversation that enables the other person to feel comfortable and speak freely. This must be balanced with a clear sense of this being an important enough topic to justify the time it will take, so you'll be creating a sense of leadership, without being controlling. Your colleague must be comfortable that you can navigate through the stages of the conversation, i.e. you know what you're doing. That will be clearer as we go along. So to summarise, your objectives at this stage include to:

- build appropriate levels of rapport, to make sure the other person feels comfortable they can have the conversation in a natural way
- create the appropriate climate for the conversation, for example professional warmth
- create a sense of leadership, i.e. they are in safe hands.

The following dialogue begins an off-line coaching conversation between Sally and her manager. As we'll use this conversation to illustrate each stage of the Coaching Path, you might like to imagine yourself as the manager.

Manager   So Sally, hi, how are you – how're things?

Sally   Yes, fine thanks, settling in nicely I think.

Manager   How do you like the new layout? You got a spot by the window I see.

Sally   Yes, it's great, I much prefer it.

Manager   Yes, I think all of us being in one place is great. Good, so, OK, we've got about 30 minutes for this, haven't we?

Sally   Yes, it might not take that long, but I booked the slot just in case.

Manager   That's fine. Let's get started, shall we?

As you can see, the manager is simply greeting the team member in an appropriate way, and when it feels natural, moving the conversation on to the task at hand. In all these examples we'll reduce the dialogue as much as possible, to stick to the key points. In real life a conversation would likely contain much more small talk or general chat, but it's less helpful here.

Stage 2: Identify clear topic and goal

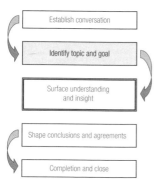

This next stage creates a sense of direction and purpose for the conversation, so that as the coach you know where you need to be heading. Remember, in this type of conversation (off-line, where the coachee/subordinate has the objective for the conversation), the manager needs to identify objectives for the conversation from what the subordinate says. So your objectives at this stage include to:

- encourage your colleague to 'own' the session by declaring what they want to get from it

- identify the purpose and topic for the session in sufficient detail to enable you to facilitate the conversation towards an effective outcome

- establish the conditions of an effective conversation, for example we'll know when we're on track and when we've wandered into a pointless digression

- create a sense that 'success is possible' or 'solution focus', i.e. we're here to work something out and this is where we will get to

- identify an 'end point' for the conversation, i.e. know when you've met the objectives.

Here you are surfacing your colleague's *topic* for discussion and also their *goal* for the conversation. That might be something fairly easy for you to do, for example if they are well prepared and feeling clear. Or it might be something you need to help them get clear about before you can begin an effective discussion. It's worth mentioning that you have an important balance to maintain at this point. That balance is between being effective and not frustrating the person in front of you, who might be eager to launch into a topic that they want to 'get off their chest'. At this stage you need a 'star to guide you' rather than an exhaustive detailed description of their agenda.

The following dialogue maps the stages between a goal that is too vague and one that has just enough clarity for you to navigate forwards.

Manager   So, what would you like to talk about?

Sally   Well, it's the whole situation with the team and recruitment we've got right now. To be honest, it's beginning to be a real concern.

So here you have a vague (broad) topic and not much of a goal for the conversation. While Sally is likely to be ready to begin talking about her 'problem', the manager probably needs to push back a little, and gain a little more focus on the conversation. For example:

Manager   OK, specifically what is it in regard to the team and recruitment you want us to talk about?

Sally   Well, it's just the delays we're getting with hiring; it's taking too long to bring people on board and the work is piling up.

So now we're clearer about the topic for the conversation, but we still have no goal to work towards. Depending on how Sally seems – for example calm, flustered, frustrated, etc. – you may decide that you need to proceed to the next stage (surface understanding) to allow her to speak. Your risk is that the conversation will simply become a 'complaining session', where Sally assumes that by discussing the situation with you it will simply 'get solved' in some way (maybe by you perhaps?). So let's risk a further challenge.

Manager   Right, so that's something we need to work through. Thinking about the next 30 minutes, what do you want to get out of this conversation?

Sally   Well, I guess I want to tell you about what's been going on, and maybe get some ideas as to what else I can do.

Notice how the responsibility for the conversation and its outcome is still firmly with Sally. The manager is working to maintain rapport and show support – 'That's something we need to work through' – while still encouraging Sally to own the conversation. For some managers this will be a challenge, as they may judge this lack of involvement by themselves as 'unhelpful'. Actually, in the longer term it's more helpful to Sally, as she learns to solve life's problems and feel confident about doing that. If at any time the manager needs to step in and 'rescue' Sally, they can. But remember that when you rescue someone you make a victim out of them in the same moment. When we are a victim we feel less powerful, as if something is happening *to* us. A more powerful posture to act from is the assumption that

> when you rescue someone you make a victim out of them

we are the cause of our experience and are able to change that experience ourselves. As a manager you can encourage others to adopt this more powerful posture by assuming that they are able to make a difference in their circumstances themselves, without the need to be 'rescued'.

brilliant tip

Ask people to arrive prepared

Your one-to-one meetings with subordinates will be easier to coach when the subordinates arrive with an objective or purpose, accepting that what they get from the meeting is largely up to them. So try asking them to arrive with topics that they want to discuss and some objectives for each topic. It's a great way to get people acting more powerfully. When they arrive for a conversation prepared, they also begin from a more mature posture, for example 'Here's what I want to get from my time with you' (instead of 'I thought we'd just chat some stuff through and see what happens').

So now that we have both a topic and a goal for the conversation, we can progress to the next stage: surface understanding and insight.

Stage 3: Surface understanding and insight

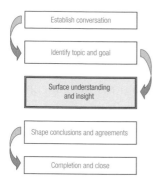

This is perhaps the most important stage in our Coaching Path, as it is where the core coaching skills come into play. It is also the heart of a coaching conversation, where your effective listening, questioning and observations or challenge enable the person to surface their thoughts and arrive at their own conclusions and decisions. The simple process of enquiry, i.e. being listened to, is also therapeutic as we are given space to 'get things off our chest' and perhaps feel better for having expressed emotions such as confusion or frustration. Your key objectives at this stage are to:

● surface a mutual understanding of the situation, issue or challenge (for example, what is the issue, what's causing the issue, what's important about the issue?)

● increase the self-awareness of the individual, in relation to the situation being discussed (for example, how might they be affecting the situation?)

● help the other person reflect objectively on the situation, i.e. express confusion or frustration, and then move on to a more impartial, balanced view

● help the person form conclusions, realisations or insights arising from clearer thinking

● create more of a focus towards solution (for example, what would be better than this, or how do you want this situation to be instead?).

---

brilliant tip

Enquire to reveal understanding (not to help you 'fix')

Remember that we are enquiring with the intention of understanding rather than enquiring in order to fix, solve or instruct.

While enquiring merely to 'understand' may seem like a pretty
pointless task, it is actually where the magic of coaching reveals
itself. When someone is asked to paint a full picture of their own
problem or challenge, they are often able to think more clearly
and rationally as a result. As they hear themselves speak, they
form realisations about the situation and also about themselves in
relation to that situation that would otherwise have lain hidden.
It's a little like decluttering someone's thoughts for them – from
a clearer perspective they can make more sense of a situation.
Sometimes it's simply a matter of emptying our heads of confused
static so that a clear signal can be heard!

Here's how the process of enquiry might sound in our conversation with Sally. Again, we've reduced the conversation right
down to keep it simple to read.

Manager   Right, so can you tell me a bit more about the
            situation?

Sally   Yes, it's quite straightforward. We've sent requests
            in to HR for two new people four weeks ago and
            so far they haven't even started first interviews.
            They're saying they're really busy with the year-
            end pay reviews. It's ridiculous.

Manager   OK. How does that impact on you and the team?

Sally   Well, immediately it's not too bad – we've still
            got Margaret here until the end of the month,
            but when she leaves we're really going to feel the
            pressure.

Manager   OK, so once Margaret leaves, then what happens?

Sally   Well, then we've got to find a way of coping with
            her workload and also a way of taking over the
            new product-reporting work that's being passed
            over from Marketing.

> *Manager* Right, I can see why you'd want to tackle this now, before it becomes a real issue.
>
> *Sally* Exactly. It's going to be a mess if we don't do something soon.

As you can see, the manager is gently building the facts of the situation, getting clear and helping Sally to focus on the key facts. The manager is also demonstrating empathy ('I can see why you'd want to tackle this now') to acknowledge her concern. Let's continue.

> *Manager* So what have you already done about this?
>
> *Sally* Well, I've been chasing HR about it, but they seem to be holding all the cards. I spoke to them yesterday and they still hadn't set a date for first interviews.
>
> *Manager* First interviews?
>
> *Sally* Yes, they like to do the first round of vetting candidates before they get to us. Once they've seen people they pass them over to us.
>
> *Manager* So where are they in that process?
>
> *Sally* Well, apparently they've got at least three candidates they think we'd be interested in, but they still haven't arranged to see them.

So by now your problem-solving skills may have leapt into gear and you think you've spotted a solution, i.e. remove the 'blocking factor' of HR and get Sally to interview the candidates first.

But remember, we are committed to Sally's own ability to come up with her own way forward. Plus there may be more we still need to hear, before jumping to a conclusion.

> *Manager* OK, so let me just confirm what I think you're saying: that we need to hire more people quickly, to cope with Margaret leaving at the end of this month, plus to take on the additional work from Marketing.

Sally   Right.

Manager HR have some candidates but they want to vet them first, and they haven't yet arranged to see them.

Sally   Yes, and if you're thinking why not let us speak to them first, it's because they haven't sat the IQ tests. If the candidate passes the IQ tests they're then asked to sign a data protection agreement. HR won't let them speak to us until they've signed it.

Notice how the manager uses a gentle summary with positive effect, before continuing to enquire further. We now have a fuller picture and one that is useful to surface. If the manager had acted on a 'fix-it' instinct earlier, their 'simple solution' (remove HR from the process) may have been rejected as an impractical suggestion. And remember, it's Sally who will benefit the most by finding her own solution. Let's continue.

Manager So what are your options?

Sally   Well, we could insist on seeing them before HR do and get the candidates to sign the data protection form ourselves, but it still won't get us the people in time. Because even if we said yes to a candidate, getting references and checks on them will still take around a month, maybe longer.

Manager Hmm, so that's not going to sort it.

Sally   No – certainly it's not going to keep us covered in the short term.

Manager OK, so let me just check, what is the real issue here you want to fix?

Sally   Well, I'm just thinking, there are two different
            issues aren't there? There's Margaret leaving and
            there's the new workload. We can deal with either
            of those situations for a short time, but not both
            at once. For example, if Margaret stayed on for a
            few weeks we could cope, or if we could push back
            the new workload coming in from Marketing, we
            could let her go.

Manager So what do you think?

Sally   Well, I'm thinking I need to look into both of
            those options, to see what's possible.

As you can see, the conversation has taken a slightly different
turn, now Sally has got clearer. You'll also notice that the conversation has gone from one of 'no possibility' ('It's a mess') to
having more of a feeling that there might be a potential solution
('I need to see what's possible').

Now that we have a clearer picture of both the issue and Sally's
options, let's go to the next stage.

 **brilliant** tip

Withholding information or giving advice?

While the manager should avoid giving quick solutions, if they know
of any information that is relevant to a subordinate's issue then
they need to declare it: for example, 'Did you realise that Marketing
are making some people redundant?' We don't want to withhold
information; we simply want to reduce our influence on someone's
decision-making process.

Stage 4: Shape conclusions and agreements

Here we want to start to pull the conversation together and help Sally shape her ideas into an appropriate way forward. In any coaching conversation the 'appropriate way forward' may range from an agreed set of actions with timescales to a much looser plan of 'go and have a think'. As coach you will decide on how much rigour and detail to encourage, according to both the topic that has been

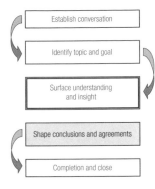

discussed and also the individual with whom you are discussing it. For example, if you know the other person is a mature individual who is able to act upon commitments, then if they say 'I'm going to go away and look at the figures – I'll get back to you', that may be enough. Or if the topic of the conversation has been highly personal (for example 'Am I in the right job?'), then an agreement to 'go away and think' may be absolutely appropriate. But if what we're discussing is time-related or we need clarity, then 'I'll come back to you on Friday morning by 9 a.m. with the document' might be needed.

So in this fourth stage of shaping conclusions and agreements, your objectives are to:

- provide a useful summary of where the individual has reached, i.e. their conclusions and ideas

- help the individual to surface any remaining conclusions or ideas that are useful

- help the person to decide on a way forward, for example actions, next steps, etc.

- challenge any false barriers or limited thinking

- create a sense of a better future (for example, how will this benefit you?) and so motivate the person to act.

Let's continue our scenario with Sally.

Manager OK, let's try and pull this together then. So you're suggesting that if you split the two issues – Margaret leaving and the impending workload from Marketing – then it may be simpler to deal with.

Sally Yes, we can cope with one but not with both, at least for a while.

Manager Right, and you're going to find out how possible it might be either to keep Margaret on for a while or to delay the new work coming in.

Sally Yes, it's certainly worth a try.

Manager Yes, I think it probably is. And I guess I'm still left wondering, what are you going to do about the longer-term solution of hiring more people?

So you'll notice that the manager is happy to support Sally to pursue the short-term 'fixes' but also wants to challenge the remaining issue of what happens longer term. I'll add that because the manager has been in the role of coach or facilitator for the conversation, this apparent oversight is actually very easy to spot. Because the manager hasn't been trying to 'figure things out' or create ideas, they are able to maintain a much clearer view of the conversation. Let's see how this continues.

Sally Yes, I know, I really need to get to grips with those guys, don't I?

Manager [laughs] Probably – what are you thinking of doing?

Sally Well, for a start I need them to commit to some firm deadlines. I do think there's an option for us to see people first – we can do the data protection form, and we can even arrange the meetings ourselves if we have to.

Manager What difference will that make, do you think?

Sally	At a minimum, we'll tighten the whole process. If we're really smart, we'll probably shave around three or four weeks off the hiring period.
Manager	How will HR react, do you think?
Sally	Well, if I can do it in the right way I think they'll welcome me with open arms.
Manager	The right way?
Sally	[laughs] Yes, you know, make it look like taking something off their plate during a very busy period or something.
Manager	[smiling] Ah, I'm sure you'll charm them into agreement.

So again you can see the manager is using a 'light touch' to help Sally plan her own way forward. In reality the manager may decide that for the sake of clarity they want to summarise the three actions (Margaret, Marketing and HR), or indeed offer further challenges or observations. But for the purposes of this example, let's assume the manager is comfortable that Sally has her way forward. We're ready to go to the final stage: completion and close.

brilliant tip

What if someone gets 'stuck' when you ask them for solutions or ideas?

First – stay calm, relaxed and focused and maintain your feelings of confidence. Your best response to someone who appears stuck will depend on what's causing their 'block'. It could be a number of reasons.

● They need reflection time – a period of gentle silence helps.

● They need a more general question, for example 'What are your options?' or 'What thoughts are you having now?'

> ● They are confused or overloaded. A gentle summary by you can give them a 'rest'. In extreme cases, offer a break.
>
> ● You haven't surfaced enough information yet. Backtrack. For example 'OK, I've heard you say that long hours, plus the travelling are the real issue – can you say a little more about that?'
>
> ● They don't believe there's a solution. Use a question that encourages possibility, for example 'You've said you want to sort this – what would 'sorted' look like for you?'

Sometimes, you'll know that they are unlikely to think of anything. Before offering your ideas, you still have other options.

● Make a gentle observation, without being too directive. For example, 'You've said that it's out of your control and also that your boss is rarely around – I'm wondering how those two are linked?'

● Acknowledge the situation. For example, 'OK, I may have led us up a dark alley, shall we pause a while? What would you like to do?'

Above all, stay open, relaxed and flexible! An uptight, frustrated coach flounders, while a calm, resourceful coach will normally create progress. Trust yourself and trust the process!

Stage 5: Completion and close

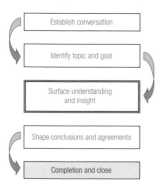

Just like opening the conversation, this stage is one you're already equipped to deal with, as really it's a professional close to the discussion. You're creating a sense of completion and also a momentum forward. You may need to refer back to the original objectives for the session, if there were several of them, just to check that everything's been covered. Your key objectives at this stage are to:

- confirm that the conversation is complete and that the other person is happy to close
- indicate that progress has been achieved
- create mutual clarity as to what happens now
- leave the subordinate feeling supported, as they go forward
- close the session in a natural way.

Nearly there! Let's see how this conversation might be drawn to a natural close.

Manager   OK, so you've got your way forward with exploring short-term options and tightening the reins on HR.

Sally   Absolutely.

Manager   Good, I think that's a really firm way forward. All right, let me just check, is there any support you need from me on this?

Sally   No, I don't think so. If I come up against anything, I'll ask.

Manager   Great. So can I just check, has this been useful?

Sally   Yes, definitely. I think I just needed to think things through.

Manager   Great. I'll be interested to hear how you get on.

Sally   [laughs] Oh, don't you worry, I'll be telling you. Thanks for your time anyway, that's great.

Manager   Oh, no problem – look we didn't even use the full slot! I'll see you soon.

So the manager is gently rounding off the conversation in a warm and supportive way. I hope you can imagine yourself doing something similar. At no time has the manager had to launch into 'instruction'; they have simply had to surface the thoughts and views of another person. Of course, it's a convenient scenario as Sally seemed intelligent and mature for most of the conversation. Here I wanted to show you the basic sequence, rather than exceptions to the sequence. For tackling tougher character types, see the brilliant tip boxes throughout the book.

CHAPTER 10

Off-line: when the manager has the topic or agenda

I n our next scenario, we're going to be using the same structure (the Coaching Path) to guide us. Let's imagine you want to speak to someone who works for you about some aspect of their work. Maybe you've become concerned about something and want to understand what's happening. Perhaps you've heard something isn't going well, or you've just got out of touch with a situation. So you arrange to see someone, in an off-line conversation. The structure of the Coaching Path would certainly help you coach that conversation. But for illustration we're going to make this one slightly more challenging. We're going to assume that there's an issue with someone's behaviour and you've decided to speak to them about it. The following example shows how to give negative feedback in a less directive, coaching style.

The Genesis project – setting the scene

You are the project manager of a project called Genesis. The project is to help the whole organisation communicate with each other more effectively. Members of the project team have been gathered from different parts of the company, for example, Sales, Marketing and Finance. Your job is to keep the project team focused on the goals and plans of the project, and support them to deliver. Yesterday you facilitated a meeting where the team got together to give updates on progress and talk through issues. You were surprised that some people appeared irritated with each other, and it affected the atmosphere around the table. Two people seemed to withdraw from participating and simply sat quietly. In particular, you felt that Robert did little to help with his manner and approach. His attitude to other team members seemed curt and even slightly hostile at times, and some of the language he used was emotive (for example, 'That's nonsense'). You have decided that giving Robert some feedback about what you saw might help. Your objectives for the conversation are to:

- describe what you saw, i.e. his behavioural responses and the impact they had
- understand more about what's going on
- agree a way forward that improves the situation, for example influence Robert's future behaviour to be more constructive.

Let's remind ourselves of our map for our journey through the conversation: the Coaching Path, as shown again in Figure 10.1.

Much of the conversation flows in a similar way to the previous scenario, with the following exceptions.

- The topic and goal will be voiced by the manager, i.e. the meeting yesterday and what the manager observed.
- The manager will be prepared to keep offering their views or feedback.
- The manager may have some specific requests to make, which contribute to the 'conclusions and agreements' stage.

Practical preparation

As the manager, you are going to tackle what may be a difficult conversation, so preparing messages and behavioural examples is important. Other preparation may include thinking about how you want to be with Robert, for example, having an open and supportive attitude (rather than being critical or judgemental). For a fuller checklist of personal preparation, see page 112.

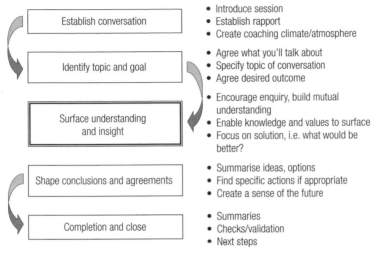

- Introduce session
- Establish rapport
- Create coaching climate/atmosphere

- Agree what you'll talk about
- Specify topic of conversation
- Agree desired outcome

- Encourage enquiry, build mutual understanding
- Enable knowledge and values to surface
- Focus on solution, i.e. what would be better?

- Summarise ideas, options
- Find specific actions if appropriate
- Create a sense of the future

- Summaries
- Checks/validation
- Next steps

Figure 10.1 The Coaching Path

Stage 1: Establish conversation

Once again, this step builds initial rapport and sets the tone for the meeting. It's also about the manager creating a sense of relaxed leadership in the conversation, i.e. believing 'I can facilitate us through this conversation (I know what I'm doing)'. In our new scenario, let's see how that might sound.

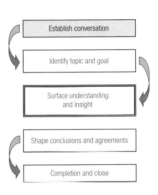

Manager	Hi Robert, thanks for doing this at short notice. Are you OK for time?
Robert	Yes, kind of – I've got another meeting in an hour, but I'm not running that one or anything.
Manager	Well, I hope not to make you late for that. An hour seems plenty of time – let's see how we go, shall we?
Robert	Yes sure, fire away.

Notice how the manager is voicing support for Robert in a respectful way: 'I hope not to make you late for that'. Robert may know that something's not quite right, and be unconsciously preparing himself: 'Yes sure, fire away'. By ignoring signs of underlying defensiveness or tension, those feelings often disappear. So the manager keeps a relaxed tone and does not react to any tension Robert may be displaying. The manager is also careful to put their own feelings about what happened in the meeting to one side. Remember, what the manager saw in the meeting yesterday was Robert acting rudely and mildly aggressively, and the manager may have been annoyed by that. But to display any annoyance might:

> by ignoring signs of underlying defensiveness or tension, those feelings often disappear

- cause the manager to think less clearly

- portray a judgemental or superior attitude (we want an 'adult-to-adult' conversation not a 'parent-to-child' conversation)

- place Robert on the defensive, i.e. he realises he's being criticised.

Ironically, for the manager to display irritation would also mirror the very behaviour that provoked this conversation – curt manner, mild hostility. If we want to encourage maturity in others, we must first begin with ourselves. So the manager maintains an objective view and supportive tone.

When giving feedback, it's important to know how our own opinions and judgements can colour both our view of someone and the way we respond to them. When we believe someone is 'wrong' – for example in how they act – we often communicate that, either subtly or overtly. This reduces rapport and therefore feelings of trust, openness and mutual support. Once those features of a relationship are reduced, so too is our ability to influence. So try to maintain an objective view, if only to give yourself a well-rounded view of a situation.

 **questions**

Test your mood

Use the following to consider how your personal judgements affect your ability to remain relaxed and objective with someone.

Think about someone in a work situation who has done something you didn't like. Perhaps they have displayed a behaviour towards you that was difficult for you to handle. Or perhaps they have behaved towards you in a way you felt was unfair, unreasonable or just plain nasty. Use a significant example if possible – one that creates discomfort. Now ask yourself the following questions.

(Q) **How do your feelings towards this person affect your behaviour and attitude towards them?**

(Q) **How are you different with them, for example what thoughts do you have about them and how does that influence what you do or say, or even how you say it?**

(Q) **If you had to give feedback to that person about this issue – for example what they did that causes you to feel like this – how relaxed and objective could you be?**

Now think about what thoughts or feelings you would have to let go of, to remain objective and relaxed with them. For example, try 'giving up' your righteousness about the situation – the idea that you are right and they are wrong. No matter how illogical that seems, just try it. Or adopt a neutral position of 'I don't know everything about this' or 'There's more to this than I understand'. Or try 'OK, I'll ignore my feelings of right and wrong just for this exercise' (you can retrieve them later). From that more neutral, objective position, consider:

(Q) **If you assume that they have been doing the best they know (because most of us do), then think again about their actions. How does that enlarge your view of things?**

▶

> Ⓠ Let's assume you're able to be generous towards this person. If your main objective for giving them feedback included trying to understand things from *their* perspective, how would that conversation go?
>
> Ⓠ If you were to have this type of conversation, what might be the benefits?
>
> Ⓠ How do you feel about this person and situation now?

Let's continue to the next stage on the path.

Stage 2: Identify clear topic and goal

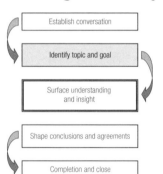

Here the path takes a slightly different turn from the one it took in the previous scenario.

Now the manager simply needs to give the topic in clear, objective terms. For example:

Manager   So, I wanted to talk about the meeting yesterday – I guess it didn't go as well as I'd hoped and I wanted to talk to you a little about that.

Robert   Right ...

Manager   I noticed that you didn't appear to be very buoyant in the meeting and I think that probably affected the tone of the meeting a little.

Robert   I'm not sure what you mean. I mean, there were a couple of times when things that were being said bugged me, but then some of what was being said was just garbage.

The manager has begun with a gentle observation – 'You didn't appear to be very buoyant' – rather than an overly specific one, such as 'I noticed you were rude to Charlotte on at least four occasions'. That's because the manager is pacing a little, to orientate Robert to the topic, before giving the specifics. The manager has come prepared with some specifics (behavioural observations), but will offer them when it's required. Robert is already preparing his defence, for example to criticise others, but it's a defence the manager will not engage with.

 **brilliant** tip

If _you_ have the topic, don't try to coach it from them!

In a conversation where the manager is clear about what they want to discuss, it's pointless trying to obtain the topic from the other person. This is a common pitfall of managers learning to coach and one that normally leads to a dead end. Because managers want to avoid being directive they forget that it's OK to own the topic of a conversation and have objectives for that conversation. So instead of being willing just to 'place the topic on the table' and give the objective feedback, the manager tries to use a non-directive style in order to 'coach' it out, which may sound like:

Manager	So, I was wondering how you thought the meeting went yesterday?
Robert	I thought it went fine.
Manager	How much of an atmosphere do you think there was in the room?
Robert	I'm not sure. I suppose I hadn't really thought about it.

Clearly the manager is hoping that Robert will open up the topic for him and perhaps even 'admit' that there was an issue. It's a flawed strategy and one that works on rare occasions. The manager should wait until the next stage (surface understanding and insight) before adopting a less directive, coaching style of enquiry.

Here's how the manager continues.

Manager   All right, can I say a little more about what I noticed?

Robert   Sure, go ahead.

Manager   I noticed that when Charlotte and Erica were giving their updates you seemed to show signs of frustration, like rolling your eyes a bit, or sighing, and at one point you told Charlotte and Erica their idea was 'nonsense'.

Robert   Well it is! Anyone knows that staff aren't going to be engaged by yet another poster campaign – we're just sick of them.

Manager   All right ... let me say what I saw after that. You see, Charlotte seemed to withdraw from the conversation, certainly she stopped talking, and Erica seemed to do the same – I think she didn't make eye contact with anyone after that.

Robert   Well, isn't that their issue?

Again the manager is retaining a balanced relaxed view, despite the signs that Robert is ready to argue. The manager is more focused on their objectives for this 'topic and goal' stage, namely to:

● offer the topic for discussion (complete)
● give objective feedback based on observation (ongoing)
● declare their objective for the conversation (ongoing, i.e. implied).

If at any time the manager allows themselves to be 'hooked' (or distracted) by comments that are less relevant to the above points, then the conversation may be side-tracked and lose direction.

Let's see how the manager continues.

Manager I guess I can see why you'd say that, but for me it
feels like all our issue. Rob, in yesterday's meeting
you didn't appear relaxed and constructive, not
how I've seen you being previously. Plus I thought
yesterday was a generally more subdued meeting
and I think your responses towards Charlotte and
Erica might have influenced that.

Robert Right.

Manager So I wanted to talk this through and find out what
your view of this is, because I want to understand
more. I also want to find a way of improving the
situation, if that's possible.

Robert OK, fine.

So the manager gives straight, open, direct messages in terms
with which Robert is unlikely to disagree. He's unlikely to disagree both because of the previous conversation that's led up to
this, and also because the manager is 'owning' the comments
from a personal perspective, for example, using phrases like 'I
thought' or 'For me it feels like'. The manager is also staying as
neutral as possible, so not saying things like 'You did this and
that's really bad' or using emotive words like 'rude' or 'arrogant'. Notice also that there are no clear 'positives' to balance
the negatives. There could be some later, if they are true, relevant and appropriate. But they are not appropriate now, as they
may confuse or reduce the important message.

What's less easy to illustrate here is that the manager must pace
the conversation in a way that enables Robert to hear what's
being said and process the information logically and emotionally. For example, if the manager rushed through the above
observations, without the appropriate pauses, there's a danger
that Robert may begin to resist the flow of the conversation
because he is struggling to react to what he's just heard. It's
important that the manager stays tuned to Robert, rather than
dashing through some pre-prepared statements.

So the manager now has their topic on the table and also a declared goal of 'understanding more and improving the situation'. Let's continue down the Coaching Path, picking up all our coaching tools as we go.

Stage 3: Surface understanding and insight

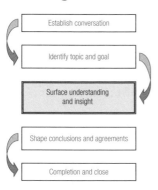

This stage now begins to match the previous scenario (with Sally). As the manager, you will be using all your skills of rapport, listening, effective questioning and feedback or observation. You want to hear more about the situation from Robert's perspective and know that he's more likely to be open if he feels you are not judging him. So you will be in simple 'enquiry' mode for much of the time. Let's continue.

Manager   So, help me understand then – how do you see the situation?

Robert   Well, it's all a mess, isn't it?

Manager   Can you say a bit more about that?

Robert   Yes. We're trying to get Marketing to engage in meaningful communications activities, like the senior management question time, and all they want to do is put up posters.

Manager   OK, what else?

Robert   I just think that Charlotte and Erica are out of their depth – they don't want to tackle the thorny issues, but just the ones that are easy to deal with.

Manager   Can you say a bit more about that?

Robert   Yes, like the fact that staff still need a clearer appreciation of the new structure and how it all fits together. Putting it up on posters is fine, but people need it explaining. We need dialogue with people – people have got questions.

Manager   So what should we be doing?

Robert   We need more of an aligned set of activities and tasks – at the moment everyone's just working from their department's perspective. Marketing know what they want, Finance has a different agenda – it's just not a coherent plan.

So the manager is gathering facts, not judging Robert's statements as good or bad, but simply letting him speak. You'll notice that Robert is gradually becoming more objective himself, as he is given space to 'get things off his chest' and perhaps clear some of his frustration. By not reacting to his frustration, the manager does not fuel it, and so gradually Robert's frustration reduces. Once Robert is calmer, he can think more objectively. If we still think Robert needs to say how he's feeling in order to 'let it go', we might ask him about it, in order to acknowledge it or help him deal with it. For example:

Manager   Can I ask how you're feeling about all this?

Robert   Yes, really frustrated. Hacked off to be honest. I thought this project was going to make a difference, but now I'm not sure it will.

Manager   So how is how you're feeling affecting your behaviour and performance right now?

Robert   Well, I'm not sure. I mean, I hadn't thought about it.

Manager   OK, well look at yesterday's meeting – how did it affect you yesterday?

Robert   Hmmph, that's obvious isn't it? I guess I'm just irritable about the whole thing.

So by acknowledging what Robert is feeling and having him consider how it's affecting him, we are tackling what may be a key issue of Robert's personal development. You may be reading this thinking, 'Yes great, but this is taking too long – why are we asking this guy what he thinks? Just tell him to improve his attitude.' Of course we could just tell him that he's got a bad attitude and he needs to improve

with coaching, we're coaching the *person* as much as the issue

it. It may actually result in his not being rude in meetings (at least for a while). But his self-awareness may remain the same, for example he'll still think the rest of the world is wrong and he's right. By telling him to change his attitude we've achieved compliance but no personal growth. Remember, with coaching, we're coaching the *person* as much as the issue.

> **brilliant** tip
>
> **A quick summary can work wonders**
>
> Part-way through a coaching conversation a brief, accurate summary from the coach can often work really well. By giving a quick summary – either of the whole conversation, or simply a few key things you've heard – both of you benefit. A well-timed accurate summary creates clarity, diffuses tension and gives people additional time to think. A summary can also refocus the discussion, or keep it on track if the conversation has digressed. My caution is that using summaries too often can slow a conversation down, or make it feel boring – so it's a great trick when used sparingly!

Let's continue.

Manager   OK, so let's look at what we've got so far. You're frustrated because the project isn't pulling together and working well together as a team.

Robert   Right.

Manager   And your frustration is causing you to act nega-
            tively towards some of the team, which is what we
            saw yesterday.

Robert   Yes, I guess so. Well, yes, maybe I was a bit snappy.

Manager   And yet you still seem really passionate about
            what the project is trying to do, because you see
            it's really needed.

Robert   I do, yes. I really do. You see, even this conversa-
            tion is annoying because now I'm seeing that the
            very thing I'm saying we should be doing is what
            I'm not doing – which is working as a team.

By a simple, relaxed summary, the manager takes the pressure
off Robert and allows him to reflect on what he's been saying.
Again, the space and the ability to detach a little have helped
Robert realise something else, namely that he's part of the problem rather than part of the solution. It's probably worth digging
one last time into Robert's thoughts, just to see what's there.

Manager   All right, so can I ask you, what thoughts are you
            having now about all this?

Robert   Well, to be honest I think I need to refocus a little.
            I've obviously let things get to me and it's not
            helping.

Manager   I'd probably agree with that. So what do you need
            to do?

Robert   I think I need to work out what my main frus-
            trations are and work on those. I don't think it's
            everything or everyone, I think it's just some key
            issues that I think aren't being dealt with.

Now, in real life we may want to continue this part of the discussion, to help surface more of Robert's ideas. We'd probably

help him work out what his main frustrations are and what are the key issues he thinks need to be dealt with.

Using simple, open questions the manager can help Robert to reflect in a useful way, for example:

- OK, so what needs to happen?
- What's important here, do you think?
- What else seems relevant to think about?

I'll add that the manager needs to be ready to give further feedback or opinion, for example 'I'm not sure that's enough'. But for the purposes of demonstration, let's move on to the next stage.

brilliant tip

Don't push too hard on actions – it may cost you equality

Sometimes we spoil the 'adult-to-adult' sense of a coaching conversation right at the end, by being pedantic or forceful when agreeing actions. For example, after coaching someone really well to create ideas around a situation, we suddenly become dominant by saying something like 'Right, so what are you going to do and by when – what am I going to see from this?'

Remember:

- Different people and situations need different levels of agreements or detail.
- You need to let go of the 'I'm in charge' attitude in favour of 'I know I can trust you'.
- Most things can be a 'longer game'. For example, if I say I'll do something and then not do it, you can pick that up at our next meeting. If over time this becomes a pattern of behaviour, you can tackle the pattern of behaviour directly, for example 'I notice that some of the actions you're committing to aren't getting done, can we talk about that?' Remember you have an ongoing relationship with the people who work with you and you can encourage maturity by assuming it first.

Stage 4: Shape conclusions and agreements

In this stage we're pulling together the key threads of the conversation and seeing what we've got: the conclusions, ideas and a way forward. In real conversations, ideas or solutions will often surface in the previous stage and then get refined in this stage. In our abridged example with Robert, this hasn't yet happened, although certainly he seems ready to think about ideas now. So let's continue.

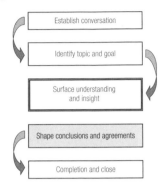

Establish conversation

Identify topic and goal

Surface understanding and insight

Shape conclusions and agreements

Completion and close

> *Manager* OK, so you feel that you've got some key issues that you feel strongly about, such as the team not pulling together, so not focusing on the main communications issues that the project is designed to address.
>
> *Robert* Yes, and it's probably just a few key things. If we sorted those, we'd do a lot of good.
>
> *Manager* I agree, and with your links into the business you're probably in a good position to see what those really are. So what are you thinking of doing?

That final question ('So what are you thinking of doing?') is quite significant, in that the manager has judged that Robert is ready to move away from discussing problems and conclusions and instead move towards a solution. The question also assumes that Robert *can* decide, which is a clear demonstration of the manager's trust in Robert's ability. That encourages a sense of empowerment in Robert. Of course, if Robert gives an idea that is either inappropriate or just plain crazy, then the manager can intervene. For example, when hearing an ill-considered plan, the manager may ask a question that causes Robert to look at the impact of the action, for example 'How will Marketing react to

that do you think?' Or if the idea is really crazy, the manager can
offer a gentle opinion: 'I think that might be outside the original
terms we've agreed for the project.' We can still influence without being parental or controlling – we don't have to say 'You
can't do that, you're not allowed to'.

Let's continue after the 'So what are you thinking of doing?'
question.

Robert   I think I'd like to call the team together again and
             tell them my frustrations. To be fair, I think many of
             us are feeling the same way – I know Dave definitely
             is. Of course, I could go in and suggest a plan for-
             wards, but it would be better if we did that together.

Manager I think that's wise – let people stay involved. OK,
             what do you see as the shape of that session?

Robert   I think we need more of an open discussion about
             how it felt when we first started the project and
             how it is feeling now. Then we need to decide on
             refocusing a little.

Manager OK, and I guess I'm still wondering, what's going
             to stop that being a session that goes the same way
             as yesterday?

Robert   Yes, well, that's down to me a bit, isn't it? I prob-
             ably need to build some bridges with some people
             and I need to think about that. Maybe it's some-
             thing that would be better done informally – I'm
             not sure.

Manager I think people would welcome that and I do think
             it would create a better feel to the next meeting.
             So what's the way forward?

Robert   Right, yes, I think I need to go away and plan that session. I need to come up with an outline or something – nothing fancy – I just can't get to it now.

Manager All right, I can see that – it's probably worth taking a little time over. So when will I hear from you again?

Robert   Give me until tomorrow – I want to speak to a couple of people.

As you can see, the manager is actually doing very little. To demonstrate the less directive posture, I've deliberately reduced the amount of input from the manager. In reality the manager might reasonably offer more views or observations, for example that:

- Robert's frustrations are impairing his ability to stay resourceful and play a really valuable role within the team.

- Robert can sometimes get 'stuck' in the problem rather than focus on solutions.

- Robert is a lot more powerful when he helps people, like Charlotte, to succeed rather than withdrawing support from them.

And again, these are all developmental points intended to support Robert, rather than instructions aimed at 'fixing' the issues. Any or all of these might comfortably sit within the 'surface understanding and insight' stage, or possibly: 'shape conclusions and agreements'. But any earlier and they may feel a little too judgemental (and create a defensive response). What's important is that they are communicated in a way that Robert feels his manager is trying to support him to be successful, rather than being critical, for example 'having a go'.

OK, nearly there, so let's wrap this up.

Stage 5: Completion and close

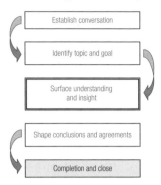

Here we are just drawing the conversation to a close while leaving the 'door open' to pick the conversation up again if we need to. Again, you've got lots of experience at ending conversations in an appropriately warm way, so here's how this one ends.

Manager   OK, that sounds like a plan. So can I ask, are we done here? Has that been useful?

Robert   Yes it has, it's a bit of a relief really. Yes, I feel a bit better about the whole thing now.

Manager   All right Rob, well thanks for that. I'll see you later then. Have a good day.

Now you may be wondering, 'OK, so where's the admission of guilt? When is Robert going to apologise to Charlotte and Erica? Is that it?' Well, here's what we need to remember.

- We are dealing with adults in an adult situation (not school, where people get punished). Our objective was not to prove Robert wrong, or to make him suffer.

- We trust Robert is a mature adult with basically good intentions: he's voiced that he needs to 'build some bridges' and we can probably assume that means with Charlotte and Erica. We've had enough of a conversation about his behaviour to make it clear that it has a negative consequence.

- If the problem behaviour continues, then we can pick up the conversation again at a later date: managing people is a longer game, remember.

I'd also add that Charlotte and Erica are also responsible for themselves, and to 'rescue' them too much may reduce or demean their position.

CHAPTER 11

Off-line:
when both the
coachee and
the manager
have things to
discuss

T his final off-line scenario builds on the previous two off-line scenarios by presenting a situation where both the manager and the subordinate have things they want to discuss. For completeness, we'll start at the beginning, and demonstrate the opening of the conversation. But in this scenario your challenge is mostly about deciding what's 'coachable' (what can be handled in a less directive style) and what's not (you simply need to confirm, or give information). My challenge is to display how most things are actually coachable and that by withholding your natural inclination to 'tell' you'll achieve more.

This time we'll imagine that you're with a subordinate for a regular update meeting. They know they need to come prepared with their objectives, and they normally bring a list of these. There are also topics you'd like to discuss, so you want to add them into the list. The meeting is with Marion, who runs a small team in a busy call centre.

Stage 1: Establish conversation

Here's the initial stage where you say hello, get comfortable and create a sense of a work-related conversation. As before, you're in the best position to judge how formal or informal you need

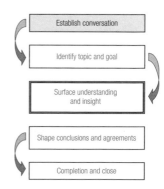

Establish conversation

Identify topic and goal

Surface understanding and insight

Shape conclusions and agreements

Completion and close

to be, but try to keep all these types of conversations as relaxed as possible. Too much 'professional-speak' can create a lack of equality in the conversation and also reduce rapport (and so openness).

Manager   Marion, hi. Gosh it's a bit cold in here, let me just adjust the thermostat. How are you, how're things?

Marion   Well, great really. Well, busy, as you know, I haven't really got time for this, but it seems ages since I saw you.

Manager   I know, it'll be Christmas next! Right, well let's get going – how long have we got for this, is it 30 minutes?

Marion   Yes, but if this room doesn't warm up I'll be out sooner than that!

As you can see, lots of familiarity and rapport. Obviously if you don't know someone too well you might be a little more formal, but you are in the best position to judge what's appropriate with each individual.

brilliant tip

Stop playing fix-it!

Coaching conversations are a challenge for managers, as they often have to listen to a problem which affects them in some way. For example, a subordinate declares they can't cope with their workload and their manager is ultimately accountable for that. So the manager wants to 'fix' the issue quickly, for example by telling the subordinate what to do, or by taking action in some way. It's crucial that the manager goes into coaching mode here, rather than 'hear problem – fix problem' mode. For the manager it may feel as though they have to stay quiet or 'sit on their hands' in the conversation. It demands both self-awareness, i.e. you need to realise you've gone into 'fix-it' mode, and also self-influence. Over time, the whole process becomes more natural, especially once you realise the benefits!

Stage 2: Identify clear topic and goal

Here we'll build the topic together, as both the manager and Marion have things they want to discuss. It's best to hear from Marion first, as she's the person responsible for her situations. We also want to keep a sense that she needs to own getting the most out of the session, and needs to come ready to work in the conversation. Let's continue the discussion.

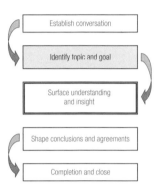

Establish conversation

Identify topic and goal

Surface understanding and insight

Shape conclusions and agreements

Completion and close

Manager All right, so let's just focus this a little then. Tell me, what would you like to get from this conversation?

Marion Well, I want to talk about three things: the latest results of our fabulous push on sales – we've just heard how we've done with that; plus the budget requirements – I want some clarity about what's needed on that. Oh, and I also want to get your input on a bit of an issue I've got with someone in my team.

Manager Great, and I'd like to pick up with you from last time about the issues we were having with customer complaints and the turnaround times.

Marion Ah yes, I've got some news on that too.

 definitions

Sympathy

The act of sharing feelings with another person. For example, if you're angry I'll get angry with you, or if you're sad, so am I.

Empathy

The ability to relate to, appreciate or understand the feelings of someone else, without necessarily taking on that emotion ourselves.

In coaching, empathy is usually more appropriate than sympathy. For example, 'I can understand this might be upsetting for you' is more appropriate than this expression of sympathy: 'That's awful, it's making me angry too.' In the empathetic example, the coach remains objective and impartial, whereas in the sympathetic example the coach becomes angry and so less objective. You want to support the individual to stay resourceful in the conversation, and helping them stay angry might not help. Occasionally, however, empathy may appear cold and sympathy is more appropriate. Once you appreciate the difference, you're in a better position to judge what's appropriate.

What's coachable and what's not?

Now, from Marion's and the manager's lists, I hope you'll notice that some of the topics seem more 'coachable' than others.

● The sales results are probably good news that Marion wants to share. Assuming that there isn't an issue with those, i.e. they're actually pretty good, then that's probably not a topic that will be helped by the Coaching Path. However, you might want to ask a few coaching questions to foster learning, such as 'So how can we build on these results going forward?'

● The budget requirements may indeed involve 'giving clarity': you're either confirming or making clear what Marion needs to do according to the process. This may be an occasion where a directive style is more appropriate, for example 'Yes, you're right, that's what we need' or 'No, we can't do that', etc. Or it might indeed be coachable, and Marion simply needs a little time and space to work out her own answers for herself. Perhaps she's wondering how much to put in the budget for training this year and is hesitant to decide. By facilitating her thought processes you can help her.

● The issue with a member of her team appears the most obviously suited for the Coaching Path. After all, Marion is managing the individual and her ability to cope with them is key to her role. If she's got an issue with someone, the best value you can add is probably to help her to decide how to tackle it.

● The customer complaints issue is also probably a coaching opportunity. It's implied that this is an issue that Marion has already discussed and the manager wants an update. By using coaching tools such as enquiry and powerful questions, the manager can support Marion to stay resourceful around that situation.

The activity of moving the conversation along the path is straightforward.

Manager Right, well I make that four things.

Marion Yes: the results, the budget, the issue with Kirsty and the customer complaints. I'll also add that those last two are sort of linked.

Manager OK, so where would you like to start?

Marion The Kirsty thing I guess – it's nagging me a bit. Can we do that first?

Manager Yes, let's talk about that then. What do you want to get out of discussing that?

Marion Well, I think I should probably sack her, but I want to know if I'm doing the right thing.

So there you have Marion's topic, the objective and goal for the conversation. It's a perfect topic to adopt a less directive posture on, as it's all about Marion's ability to deal with a difficult member of her team. There's a temptation for the manager to become involved in what might be a 'juicy issue' and give advice in a potentially dramatic situation. But by staying objective and impartial, the manager can coach. After Marion's last statement, the manager might easily choose to move on to the next stage, 'surface understanding and insight'. So let's do that.

> by staying objective and impartial, the manager can coach

Stage 3: Surface understanding and insight

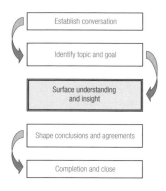

So here we move into enquiry mode around the situation with Kirsty. Remember that we're seeking to understand – surfacing Marion's thoughts, ideas and views – rather than trying to arrive at a smart solution to the situation. As always, we're assuming the answers will come from Marion.

Manager   OK, can you tell me a little more about the situation with Kirsty then?

Marion   Well, on Friday things came to a head. I overheard Kirsty being really rude to a customer on the telephone and had to take her to one side and talk to her about it.

Manager   OK.

Marion   And her attitude was the same as I'd experienced previously – she seems to lose her temper at the slightest thing and then regrets it later. She knew exactly that what she'd said to the customer was inappropriate, but once again in the heat of the moment she'd been defensive and argumentative.

Manager And you've had these discussions before, haven't you?

Marion Oh yes, several times – at least five, I'd say. That's what makes me think I need to consider letting her go.

Manager You seem a bit reluctant about that.

Here the manager is adopting a more detached perspective – which is one of the benefits of not trying to 'fix' the issue, or give any advice. Because the manager is more detached, they are able to empathise more easily, or relate to Marion's apparent 'mood'. By reflecting this back at Marion, it creates a worthwhile shift in the conversation.

brilliant tip

Coaching isn't just asking questions!

When we learn to coach we might assume that the principle 'Don't tell people what to do' means 'Get people to think by asking more questions'. Then we put those two things together and decide that a coaching conversation is a series of questions and very little else. That's not true! Asking someone lists of questions can place them (and you) under too much pressure, so remember to do all the other conversational 'stuff' like summarising, confirming, musing or 'waffle' – for example, 'Right, got it, that's quite a large piece of work then isn't it?' or 'Right ... OK ... Oh ...' Take the pressure off and let it feel natural – remember, coaching is always a conversation. The behaviours outlined in Chapter 7 on page 85 will also help to enable your coaching conversations to flow naturally.

To continue the conversation:

Marion   Well, to be fair, I am. I mean she's a nice girl, a lovely girl really, she can just be a bit immature, if you know what I mean. She just needs to calm down a bit, you know, realise it's not school and it's not a teacher that's telling her off – it's a customer who often has a genuine cause for complaint.

Manager   So what causes her to lose her temper, do you think?

Marion   [pauses] You know, I think it's that she takes things personally. It's like it's her against the customer, or even the world! It's not like she's even the one that's at fault, it's the service engineers who have often made the mistake. But you'd think to admit we've made a mistake would kill her.

Manager   So what are you thinking of doing?

Marion   Well, on Friday I honestly felt like 'enough is enough', and accepting that things just aren't going to change.

Manager   And now?

Again the manager is able to notice what isn't being said, because of their objective view of the conversation. Marion is in two minds. The manager's role is to help her decide what she wants to do.

Marion   Oh, I don't know – take her by the scruff of the neck probably! She's such a feisty character. I just feel she's got real potential, you know – she's got more about her than most people her age. Maybe she just needs some training or something.

Manager   So what are you thinking now?

That last question is what I'd call 'artfully vague', in that it leaves the potential response very broad, while moving the conversation on a little by beginning to probe for potential conclusions.

Marion   I'm not sure. I think she'd benefit from hearing how she's supposed to handle difficult customers. She could do with taking a leaf out of Neil's book – he'd make a good peacekeeper for the UN, that one.

Manager Is that possible?

Marion   You know, it probably is. I mean, we could soon hook her up to the call recording equipment and she could listen to some of Neil's calls on playback.

The manager is again doing very little except facilitating Marion's thoughts, allowing her to express her thoughts and feelings. The benefit of this is that Marion appears to be getting clearer in her own mind and making her own decisions. We're now ready to go to the next stage, 'shape conclusions and agreements'.

Stage 4: Shape conclusions and agreements

Here we are pulling the conversation together, so Marion can decide what she's got from the conversation and also be clear about what she's decided to do going forwards.

Establish conversation

Identify topic and goal

Surface understanding and insight

Shape conclusions and agreements

Completion and close

Manager All right, so what have you decided in this conversation?

Marion   [laughs] Well, I'm obviously not going to sack her, am I? I think she's my own personal challenge or something.

Manager [laughs] Hmm, well I do think it sounds like she's worth trying something different with. What are you going to do?

> *Marion*   I'm going to get her to sit next to Neil, and I'm also going to get her to listen to some of his calls. And if that doesn't work I'm going to run out screaming or something!
>
> *Manager*   [laughs] OK, so if that happens I'll know who's to blame! I do think it's a good plan though – let me know how you get on, I'll be interested to hear.

Marion has benefited from getting the problem off her chest and also finding out how she really feels, now her initial frustration has been expressed. I know that Marion and the manager had more topics for discussion, but for the purposes of illustration, we'll end it here. If we were to continue with those other topics, we'd simply pick one of the other items on the agenda and take it straight to the second stage, 'identify topic and goal'. But with this topic, we're now ready to move to the final stage: 'completion and close'.

Stage 5: Completion and close

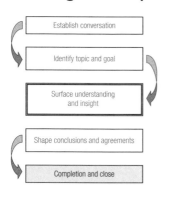

So now we're checking that it's OK to close the conversation, and then ending it in an appropriate way. Given the familiarity between Marion and her manager, it's straightforward.

> *Manager*   All right Marion, so let me just check – are we OK to close this here?
>
> *Marion*   Yes, that's fine. I'm happy with where we've got to.
>
> *Manager*   Right, well let's end there then. I guess you'll be wanting to get back.
>
> *Marion*   I am – I've got a customer call-back to do before 3 p.m. Anyway, I'll see you again. Thanks for that.

CHAPTER 12

On-line: Response Coaching

R esponse Coaching is coaching as an automatic behavioural response to any day-to-day issue, question or challenge. So when you are faced with issues or questions, instead of fixing problems you coach them instead. These issues often occur in the live operational environment as opposed to a formal (planned) coaching session. You'll remember we call this 'on-line' (and away from the workplace is 'off-line'). The issue might range from a trivial question from a junior colleague, such as 'The meeting room's double-booked, what do we do?', to a more significant 'The system's gone down and we can't process any orders'. And in these situations, a manager's coaching needs to create progress as good as, or better than, any directive instruction. So how do we coach 'on the hoof' and still make progress on tasks? Figure 12.1 illustrates a three-step model that's designed to help.

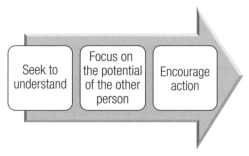

Figure 12.1 Response Coaching

Let's imagine that you're managing a team of call opera-
tives who work in a busy call centre. One of the team, Neil,
approaches you with a problem he hopes you'll solve for him:
'I've got a customer on the line who wants to return a faulty
product, but he's three days out of the 12-month guarantee
period – what should I tell him?'

You decide that this is the type of query that Neil should be
capable of answering himself. Perhaps you want to encourage
his confidence, explore his potential, or simply challenge his
routine response of 'I'll avoid taking responsibility here.'

 **checklist**

Response Coaching key principles

Here's a quick reminder of the key principles that support Response
Coaching (on-line) situations.

● This is an 'adult-to-adult' conversation, i.e. you are both mature and
equal in the conversation.

● The other person is responsible both for the issue they are surfacing and
for their actions in relation to that issue – not in a 'blame' sense, but in
being empowered to think and act.

● The other person probably has their own thoughts and ideas in the
situation, or can be challenged to create a constructive way forward for
themselves.

● You add value to the conversation by facilitating their thoughts and
ideas, using effective questions to encourage thought and offering your
observations and feedback.

● While you probably have experience and expert advice you could offer,
you would prefer they come up with solutions and so you will not give
answers until it becomes silly not to. Even then, you'll make 'gentle
offers', for example 'Can I offer a thought?'

Stage 1: Seek to understand

First, begin the process of
questioning and listening, so
you can reveal the full facts of
the situation. For example:

- So what are the key facts,
  e.g. what happened?

- What seems important in this situation?

- What else do we need to consider?

We're surfacing a clear appreciation of the situation by both the
manager and the team member. Continuing the Neil example,
during the following dialogue Neil is encouraged to 'work' in
the conversation, as the manager uses a few simple questions,
summaries and observations. This begins the conversation in a
way that allows the team member to maintain a sense of ownership. It also becomes a way of 'interrupting' a manager's old
habits, as the manager focuses on understanding, rather than
'fixing'. As usual, I've simplified the dialogue to reduce your
reading time. Here's how the conversation might sound.

Neil   I've got a customer on the line who wants to
return a faulty product, but he's three days out of
the 12-month guarantee period – what should I
tell him?

Manager All right, what are the main facts?

Neil   Well, it's a petrol lawnmower – he says he's only
used it a few times, he bought it before his garden
was actually finished. Anyway, he got it out for the
first time this year and the starter cord has snapped.

Manager So what is he asking for?

Neil   Well, he thought it was still in the guarantee period, so he was expecting us either to replace it or fix it. I've told him we might not do either – after all, it's out of guarantee.

Manager All right, anything else?

Neil   I don't know – what do you mean?

Manager Well, before we can make a decision, what else do we need to consider?

Neil   Errr. I don't know. Well I guess the issue of fairness or customer service or something ... I mean, he's only used it a few times. Plus he seems like a really straight bloke – I mean, he's not trying it on or anything.

The manager is questioning the team member in order to display the facts of the situation, to both him and Neil. The manager is doing that in a way that helps make a decision for the current issue, and also teaches Neil how to think through a similar future issue. Next time Neil has a similar situation, he's likely to 'walk through' the same process himself, for example saying to himself 'OK, to make a decision, what do I need to consider?'

Let's continue to the next stage.

Stage 2: Focus on the potential of the other person

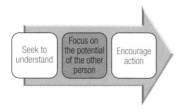

This stage requires the manager to shift their own mindset and behaviour. Here the manager assumes the person is the source of the solution. Indeed, the manager must ignore their own compulsion to 'have the answer'. In our scenario, after hearing what Neil has just said, the manager is probably very able to make a decision. But instead they must work to gain conclusions, options and actions from the *subordinate*. For example, the manager can ask:

● So what options do we have?

● All right, what are you proposing?

● What do you want to do now?

The manager is facilitating thought, helping the team member to make proposals or suggestions. Of course, the team member might not be able to think of anything, or what they do think of may be unreasonable or inappropriate. But remember, the manager has other things they can do first, before giving a direct instruction. For example, the manager can:

● offer a summary (for example, 'So he's hardly used it – and you trust him about that – and it's just the starter cord that's broken. You're concerned that we need to offer good service and you need to decide what that is')

● give an observation (for example, 'Well, you seem to think we should do something to help – what's fair, do you think?')

Here's how the dialogue might continue.

Manager So what are your options?

Neil Well, we can do nothing – tell him we can't help. Or we can offer to fix it, or even replace it. I guess we could even refund it, but that seems a bit much ...

Manager So, what's reasonable?

Neil I think we should offer to fix it really.

The manager has effectively 'walked through' a logical decision-making process with Neil that has encouraged Neil to form his own conclusion and decision. The manager has influenced Neil's thoughts, without controlling them. For example, by asking 'What's reasonable?' the manager has reminded Neil that he needs to keep his suggestion within logical commercial boundaries. This helps Neil balance a 'wonderful' solution, with a reasonable one. If we wanted to reduce the manager's influence further, we would have asked a question that was even more open, for example 'So what do you want to do?'

Stage 3: Encourage action

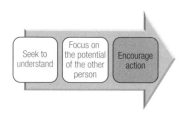

This stage creates engagement and motivates the team member to act. We're ensuring that ownership of the solution remains with them, leaving the manager to offer support if appropriate. For example, the manager can say:

● That sounds a good plan, what's the next step then?

● Is there any support from me you need with that?

● Great – it'll be good to hear how you get on.

This example is fairly straightforward, plus we need to come to a conclusion quickly (the customer is on hold, remember!). Here's a simple close to this example.

Manager   OK, so what are you going to do?

Neil   I'll tell him we'll fix it and then arrange for a service engineer to call round.

Manager   Great, sounds like a good solution for him and us – thanks for that.

This is a simple example to demonstrate the three-step Response Coaching model. The model isn't doing anything clever or complex. But it is encouraging an important shift in mindset, from fixing to coaching. As a manager, your challenge isn't to understand the model, it's remembering to use it! To coach consistently, you must be self-aware in these circumstances – and recognise when you don't need to give the answer.

But surely fixing the issue is faster?

Here's the same example where the manager chooses to 'fix it' rather than coach the situation.

Neil I've got a customer on the line who wants to return a faulty product, but he's three days out of the 12-month guarantee period – what should I tell him?

Manager All right, what are the main facts?

Neil Well, it's a petrol lawnmower – he says he's only used it a few times, he bought it before his garden was actually finished. Anyway, he got it out for the first time this year and the starter cord has snapped.

Manager So, what is he asking us for?

Neil Well, he thought it was still in the guarantee period, so he was expecting us either to replace it or fix it. I've told him we might not do either – after all, it's out of guarantee.

Manager All right, anything else?

Neil I don't know – what do you mean?

Manager OK, tell him we'll fix it, but actually we shouldn't be doing it – he is out of the 12-month period after all.

Neil OK boss – will do.

Bish bash bosh (boss) ... sorted – so where's the issue?

Some people would argue that the above exchange is shorter and the time pressure justifies simply telling Neil what to do. But remember that while this directive exchange has a time benefit, it also has a time cost, because the next time Neil gets a similar question from a customer he's likely to come back requiring the same 'Solomon' like judgement on a situation.

Neil is also likely to feel like his role is pretty low level and he's required to obtain 'permission' for even the most mundane of decisions. Neil might prefer that (for various reasons), or he may be frustrated by it, especially if he considers himself as having some potential, ambition or intelligence.

Where the manager's response is consistently a coaching one, Neil is likely to feel able to work out for himself what he should do *and* that his manager trusts him to decide. This achieves the goal of many organisations – which is to have an empowered workforce who think and act responsibly.

the goal of many organisations is to have an empowered workforce

brilliant tip

Coaching is a different kind of contribution

When you coach you're adding value in a different way, i.e. facilitating the thought processes of other people. That can take a little getting used to. Literally, you will know the answer to a situation and not offer it. That's because you've decided the benefits of developing people's thought processes for themselves is more valuable to you than a 'fast fix'. That's what we mean by 'teaching a hungry man to fish'. Over time, subordinates learn to expect this process, which can result in their stepping through the same thought process by themselves – and that's empowerment.

 **brilliant** recap

Application

Coaching principles and behaviours can be applied in a variety of everyday work situations. These can range from a formal review meeting to discuss someone's performance, to a bite-sized conversation in the queue in the canteen. Knowing how much structure and what approach to take will enable you to choose the type of coaching that's appropriate and effective. The Coaching Path and the Response Coaching models are designed to help you in any situation you might encounter. Much of your challenge is to stay self-aware, for example of your own compulsions to 'help' or 'fix' the situation, by giving quick and easy answers. When you (and your colleagues) experience the benefits of your coaching, then coaching becomes a behaviour you'll naturally want to use more often.

PART 4

Action

CHAPTER 13

Taking your learning forward

I n this final chapter we'll consider where you are now in terms of your ability to coach. We'll also focus on the journey ahead as one that takes you towards coaching being a natural and straightforward thing to do in your work situations. As usual, I'll offer routines for you to work through, to help equip you for your travels. I will also be asking you some questions, and it may help to write your answers down. And of course I'll be leaving you with an invitation to return – this book is one that wants to work hard for you, so please allow it to do just that!

Where are you now?

By now, I hope you've found enough information and guidance to enrol you in the opportunity of coaching: perhaps as a general style you could develop at work, or simply as something you could use with certain people or situations. Your challenge now is to continue your journey and blend coaching principles naturally into what you do every day. Here's where you might be, in terms of thoughts and feelings.

> your challenge is to blend coaching principles naturally into what you do every day

- I know it's something I need to do and I do understand the general concept, but I'm not sure I can do it naturally in all situations. I'm a bit worried what people might think if I suddenly start behaving differently.

- I've been trying to remember to do this stuff, and sometimes I do – but to be honest it's too easy to slip into my old style of managing, especially when things get hectic.

- I'm really interested in doing it, but I just can't see where I'm going to apply it.

- I've got it! I'm already doing it – it suits a lot of my personality and style anyway – so I'm just going to build on what I was already doing.

- Some days I think I've got it, others I don't – I'm having good days and bad ones.

There is no 'right' place to be in as you read this: wherever you are is wherever you are. Which is an odd yet hopefully relevant statement! Remember that if any of the above are true in any way, then you're in a perfect position to move forward from there. And don't forget that before you picked up this book you were functioning with an existing set of skills that are all still with you. Your opportunity now is to build on those skills and to create more flexibility around people and situations.

🌟 brilliant questions

Where are you now?

Use the following questions to consider what you want to focus on now. Write your answers down if that helps.

> **Q** Of all the ideas and information in this book, what are the things that really resonated with you the most?

> **Q** What single idea 'bothered' you the most, for example you didn't like it, were bugged by it, etc.?

Q **If you could change one thing about your style at work, what would it be?**

Your responses to the above questions can help you identify what are the key opportunities for you to learn new behaviours and get better results. For example, maybe the idea of having to develop rapport with people really irritated you as you felt it was all too 'touchy-feely'. Perhaps you're bothered by this because currently you're uncomfortable with having to relate to (or connect with) people in this way. I'd say that your frustration is actually pointing to a potential weakness in your managing style and so is an opportunity to learn.

Where would you like to get to?

Having reflected a little on where you are now, you can now consider how far you'd like to develop your coaching skills. You may relish the opportunity to adopt coaching as a consistent way of behaving at work. Or it might be that to become a 'complete coaching manager' just isn't for you. But maybe you've recognised that to be a better listener might help, or that to ask some smart questions in situations would add value. As always, you are the best judge.

brilliant questions

Where would you like to get to?

Consider the following questions to help you decide what benefits are available to you now.

Q **If you coached people around you more often, what would be different?**

Q **Of the skills you've read about (building rapport, listening, questioning, flexible styles of influence and giving feedback), which would make the biggest difference, if you got better at it? What would improve?**

▶

Ⓠ What career goals do you already have? Which of the coaching skills
can help you achieve those?

Now imagine that whatever you decided you wanted has come true. For
example, it's over a year from now and you've been using coaching skills for
a while – what's changed? Think both about how things might feel and also
how other people might be different, for example how they might react to
you. Write down any thoughts that occur.

How are you going to get there?

Having thought a little about your destination, let's look more
closely at the journey ahead. Think about the things you'll be
doing to learn the skills you've decided you want. Now write
down a list of those things, keeping it simple and practical.
For example:

● I'm going to practise being 'present' to people, to improve
my listening.

● I'm going to tell my team to stop expecting me to give them
answers all the time.

● I'll be holding more regular one-to-one meetings.

● I'll be asking more questions in conversations.

● I'll be asking for feedback on my management style.

What might stop you?

As we endeavour to create change, life will normally challenge
us with barriers or obstacles to overcome. By thinking a little
about what might stop you from learning the skills you want,
you can be ready to move through anything standing in your
way. Perhaps that's your own laziness in a situation, e.g. wanting to give quick and easy answers rather than work harder to
help someone get to their own. If you know that you have the
tendency to 'do the easy thing' in a situation, at least you can

spot it when it crops up and say 'Aha – I knew I'd want to do this – now, am I going to let it stop me?'

? brilliant questions

What might stop you?

Reflect on the following to help you identify your potential barriers to progress.

(Q) What has stopped you so far from adopting the coaching behaviours, for example as you were reading this book?

(Q) Of the skills you've read about (building rapport, listening, questioning, flexible styles of influence and giving feedback), which are you going to find most tough to tackle? Why?

(Q) What's the main thing that might stop you from bringing coaching skills into your everyday style?

When you've got answers to these questions, think a little about what you might do to overcome those barriers, writing your thoughts down if that helps. And sometimes it's enough just to acknowledge the barriers as, somehow, recognising them diminishes them.

brilliant tip

Support for your learning

Spend a little time thinking about what support you need for your journey of learning and development. Maybe you like reading, or listening to audio books, or maybe you're more action based and like attending training courses. Maybe you learn from other people, such as a colleague or mentor or coach. Some people like to keep a learning diary, writing down their thoughts and experiences to help them focus on a topic. We learn in different ways, so be creative and decide how you will support and sustain your learning going forward.

 recap

Taking your learning forward

So you've reflected a little on where you are now, where you'd like to be and also upon the journey ahead. By understanding how you'll benefit from developing these skills further, I hope you're motivated to tackle any of your challenges along the way. The simple skills of building rapport, listening, questioning, flexible styles of influence and being able to offer constructive feedback will equip you not only to coach, but to operate successfully in whatever role or career you choose. I hope that this book has supported the work that you do – please revisit any time, and I wish you good luck with your coaching!

Index